GUIDE TO CROSS-COUNTRY SKIING
IN NEW ENGLAND

Pick a place and
lets go !
— Rick + Aunt
Christmas 1987

GUIDE TO CROSS-COUNTRY SKIING IN NEW ENGLAND

by

Lyn and Tony Chamberlain

Photography by Janet Knott

The Globe Pequot Press

Chester, Connecticut 06412

for Earl and Hobie,
with our love

Updated Winter 1986–87

Copyright © 1985 by The Globe Pequot Press

Library of Congress Cataloging-in-Publication Data

Chamberlain, Lyn.
    Guide to cross-country skiing in New England.

    Includes index.
    1. Cross-country skiing—New England—Guide-books.
2. New England—Description and travel—1981- —
Guide-books. I. Chamberlain, Tony. II. Knott, Janet.
III. Title.
GV854.5.N35C45 1985   917.4   85–17561
ISBN 0-87106-856-7 (pbk.)

Manufactured in the United States of America
First edition/Second printing, December 1986

Contents

Introduction

This book has been assembled with the single purpose of enhancing the pleasure of cross-country skiers in their sport by pointing them in certain directions. It by no means pretends to be a skiing bible. It does not get especially technical in questions of technique, and it even waffles on the question of whether to buy waxable or waxless skis. Its waxing approach is clearly for the lazy. It will not tell you how to skate or double-pole. It will not even attempt to suggest that descending steep turny downhills on Nordic skis will ever be anything but a terror for you.

No, these pages have been assembled by a couple of folks who love the sport of skiing in all its facets, who love the rural reaches of New England and who hardly miss a winter weekend getting there, and who now share with you a few of the things they have found out.

About This Book

This is a guidebook for skiers and has been written for the skier, not the ski area. That is to say, the descriptions of ski areas herein are as faithful to the experience as we could make them. Prospective skiers may be influenced by what they read here to try this touring center or that one because it rings a particular note of appeal. That is the intent of this book.

Certain information may be lacking. Price, for instance. As you look at the statistical top half of an area's description, you will not find price. That is only partly because we hope this book outlives the price changes of one or two years. More to the point, within a 95-percent range of all the areas, prices are all about the same: they fall between $3 and $6 for a day's trail pass. Rental equipment ranges from $8 to $12.

Two other near universals: There are no areas where children are unwelcome; there are no areas where pets are welcome.

Unlike many Alpine areas that make a selling point of the fact that they operate a nursery for toddlers, this is hardly ever the case with Nordic areas. Exceptions will be noted in the narrative section in the lower half of the description.

Dogs, leave them home. Period. You may have a romantic picture in your mind of coursing through the pristine woodlands with Rover leaping along beside you. Save this for woods and wilderness touring of your own making. But when visiting a commercial touring center, especially one with groomed and trackset trails, leave the beasties home. Aside from ruining the track as they run along, dogs will inevitably blunder into the path of another skier (especially on double tracks), send that skier out of control, or worse, unwittingly knock him over. No fair. Dogs stay home.

A word about trail difficulty. The nomenclature has changed over the years and the current terms "easiest, more difficult, most difficult" have been thoughtfully chosen by the Professional Ski Instructors of America (PSIA). They replace the earlier "beginner, intermediate, expert" for two important reasons. First, these earlier terms were an attempt to describe the skiers who should use such trails, not the trails themselves. Secondly, no one knows exactly what the terms really mean. What is the difference, please, between an "advanced intermediate" and a newly arrived "expert," or an "experienced beginner"?

The new terms attempt to describe, in a relative way, the difficulty of a particular trail. If a trail system offers "most difficult" terrain, that means it is more difficult than its second-degree terrain, "more difficult." This latter is more difficult than the "easiest" terrain at the particular area, but not necessarily all areas.

The trail-grooming entry attempts to let a skier know what sort of a playing surface to expect. A groomed trail means that some device or other—perhaps just a snowmobile—has passed over the raw snow and packed it down, making it generally a bit faster and easier to ski than non-groomed snow. A trackset is just what it says. By pulling another device over the snow, a firm, well-defined track is set to ski in. This makes the skiing easier, faster, and is sought by folks who like to "run" on their skis. On tracks it is easier to concentrate on what your body is doing rather than the terrain.

Double trackset means at least two tracks have been set, one beside another. This works just like automobile traffic (with the exception of one-way loops). Faster skiers pull out to pass slower ones; skiers from opposite directions pass without having to get out of a track. There is nothing less courteous, by the way, than two companion skiers coming abreast of one another, using both tracks, and forcing a skier from the opposite direction out of his right-hand track. Very gauche, but it is mentioned here because it happens. Probably new converts from Alpine skiing.

Under instruction, PSIA-certified stands for Professional Ski Instructors of America. If the notation is made this way it means that your instructor has had to prove to other professional instructors that he knows what he is doing, and teaches according to a method recognized and used by all others in PSIA. It is an indication that you will have a skilled teacher.

The converse, however, is decidedly not true. Merely because a teacher is non-certified is no indication that he is not just as good as a certified instructor. So don't weigh this catagory too heavily, except to note whether any instruction is available.

On rentals, we have noted where possible how many sets are available. Some areas simply chose not to tell us how many they had, while others gave us detailed rundowns on their state-of-the-art binding systems. One rule of thumb anywhere, however: If you're going to rent, show up early. This is obviously true of the busier areas, but should be standard practice anyway. Arriving later may mean you're forced into compromises like skis too long and boots too small. No fun. One alternative to explore is renting equipment at the ski shop near your home and taking it with you. This way you'll also avoid that brutal Saturday morning crush in the rental store.

To know where you're going, use the state map. Find the number of the touring center you are visiting. The number refers to the map index giving you the page number where the area is described. Between the description in the book and the routes on the map, most places will be easy to find. But frequent visitors to New England's rural reaches should also be armed with full-scale, detailed road maps.

Two final notes: First to skiers, this book is written for you. Write and give us feedback. Tell us where you think we blew it. Maybe we glowed too much, or not enough. Perhaps you found some feature worth noting at an area that we missed. The only way we'll ever know is if you drop us a line at The Globe Pequot Press, Box Q, Chester, CT 06412.

To the touring centers, if you have made changes, improvements that we should know about, or if we have overlooked an important feature of your center that you feel should be included, likewise, drop us a line.

And to any touring center not included herein, understand that this book is not advertising. No touring center has paid to be listed in this book. If you wish to be considered for a future edition, please write and let us know you're out there.

All that said, we repeat the hope that this guide to skiing in New England will accomplish our single goal of contributing to the pleasures of the marvelous sport of cross-country skiing.

A Few Misconceptions

In the autumn of 1984 Russian archeologists found a ski near Soviet Georgia carbon-dated to an age of 4000 B.C. That find displaced by a thousand years a Norwegian ski believed to be the oldest in existence. What ever competitive spirit may exist over what country owns the oldest ski, the real point is that in frigid climes man has probably been on skis as long as he has used his feet. Beyond mere amusement or exercise regimen, the simple fact is that skiing is the fastest, easiest, and most natural way to travel over the snow-covered earth.

Not that the sport needs a defense. Indeed, cross-country skiing, with all its names and variants—ski touring, Nordic, Norpine, Telemarking—is here for a good long stay. It has that winning formula: cheap, simple, healthy, and fun. Its importance to a modern human who increasingly searches for ways to bring nature into his recreational and exercise life makes skiing nearly as significant as it was to ancient man.

For a decade in our country, cross-country skiing has redoubled several times in popularity. The sport is now an established, solid, growing, thriving, and incredibly healthful endeavor. But a few old misconceptions still remain.

Number One: It's too much work.

Well, for starters, how much work is too much work? Some people believe cross-country skiing is in the running family, that if they can't imagine themselves jogging five miles a day, then they're disqualified from cross-country skiing.

Not so. Running, aside from the well-documented jarring involved, is an all-or-nothing sort of regimen. That is, either one is running or one is not running. If one is not running he is walking or standing still. If he is running, no matter how slowly, he is under terrific stress—the whole point of the sport. His only way out is to stop, and then he is not running anymore.

Skiing is very different in that regard. In its recreational mode it is much more like bicycling. One can either bike at 100 beats a minute in the Tour de France, or one may coast and cruise. Pump five strokes, then let the legs rest as the eyes take in the countryside. Skiing can be done exactly this way, from a vigorous running pace to a leisurely cruise with lots of coasting. To be utterly frank, though, if an easy to moderately-paced bike ride is too much work for you, then, yes, cross-country skiing is probably not for you, either.

Number Two: It's boring.

This is easier. Anyone who gets bored with the winter wilderness outside those walls, with the dazzle of sun on snow-white and evergreen, is simply bored with himself, bored with life, we think. Cross-country skiing won't help.

**Number Three:
"If you can walk you can cross-country ski."**

We have seen too many people disappointed by this amiably misguided notion to let it go unanswered. There is a minimal amount of truth here to be sure. The phrase is generally repeated to assure novices that Nordic skiing has nothing of the slam-bang recklessness they perceive in downhill skiing.

In some ways this is true, but it is only true because you begin to cross-country ski on flat terrain. Move the legs in a walking sort of way, and the skier will move forward. No problem. But somewhere along the way one of two things will happen. The new skier will eventually encounter the need to go up, down, or sideways—situations that call for more concentration than your average after-dinner walk. Or, as he steps along, another skier will go by him on the trail so fast he looks motor-driven. Actually, this skilled skier looks like a little machine put together with elastic bands and pendulums: everything rhythmic, easy, and—oh Lord!—so fast.

Once the new cross-country skier sees what real skiing is like, he endeavors to go faster, mainly because the faster you go on skis the more fun you have. But it takes more skill to go fast, some practice and experience. It is here cross-country skiing departs the realm of walking. Oh, it is still as leisurely as the skier wants it to be. But once the bug gets into the advanced beginner's head that springing across flat tracks at 15 miles an hour looks like fun, well, in our judgment that is the real gateway to cross-country fun. And it sure isn't walking then.

How to get from here to there?

That's the easiest question in the book. Take a lesson. Get a certified professional to teach you. Not in big doses. But half an hour here, half an hour there. The practice in between times—pleasant miles under the skis—is the key to progressing. Keep in mind, however, that you do not have to progress, but you will most likely want to improve your skills. You need not ever feel compelled to be anything beyond a woods-walker, an air-sniffer, and birdsong-listener. Indeed, we should all remember this is primal in the joy of ski touring.

We have seen at least two distinct kinds of malaise develop over this matter of skiing proficiency or skill. One day we took a friend skiing for the first time. He was an athlete, a marathon runner, and a sometime Alpine skier in terrific physical condition. As our appointed date at the Weston Ski Track approached, we made the mistake of sloughing off my friend's real concerns about his first experience with skinny skis.

Would it feel awkward? Would he fall down a lot? Hurt himself?

"Are you kidding?" we would say. "An athlete in your condition, who has good downhill experience? You'll pick it up like that."

Our afternoon at Weston was a disaster. Not that our friend fell all over the place, hurt himself or hyperventilated in fatigue, mind you. No, cross-country skiing was merely a maddening frustration for him.

At the Weston track there are always a few expert runners in training who make 20 miles an hour over the flats look easy. And of course, given our advanced promotion, along with our friend's expectation that he could master Nordic skiing immediately, well . . . disaster is the word. He teetered unsurely, tried with determination to take off at top speed, and just never got over feeling off balance and rather foolish. A conspicuous failure. The worst of it was he wanted to look like the experts, wanted to go just as fast. He thought he should be able to, and just could not understand why it didn't come to him at once. He has not been skiing since.

The second malaise came from someone who did not want to go fast, who did not want to run through courses, who cared not a fig about double-poling and less about skating. If a hill looked less like a challenge than a chore, she would opt for the route around it. Or at least she would climb it slowly and under protest.

What she loved most about skiing was the solitude, the utter porcelain beauty of the winter landscape, the tracks of wild animals crossing the trail, the difference between white and silver birch. This woman was (dubiously) blessed to have a husband and two sons who were jocks. Every minute on skis was a contest with each other or any surrounding bit of landscape. Every ski trip became, rather than a tour in remote wilderness beauty, a challenge. Where she did not want to run up a hill, they prodded her with the old, "It'll feel good when you get up there."

The challenges the males of this family found fun and exciting were merely obstacles to the woman's enjoyment. She had a feeling they all moved so fast they were not possibly taking in their surroundings.

But, you say, understanding this is merely human courtesy or sensitivity.

Yes, of course, as was the first case. Still, these are two examples we've seen played out repeatedly. Which is why we invariably suggest that the beginner go straight to a qualified professional instructor. The pro will find out what you know about skiing, what you expect from the sport, and where you want to go. And, he can reassure you that you needn't go anywhere you do not choose to go. He will encourage you to progress at your own pace so you do not frustrate yourself trying to accomplish things you're not ready for.

Friends and relatives who know something about the sport can be helpful, but the dark side is they often are not. Often, in fact, they make the cardinal mistake of trying to teach too much, and this leads to serious malady. Go with the pro. Learn a couple of things every so often to work on when you're skiing at your leisure. And—most important at times—declare yourself to those around you. Don't be bullied into skiing over your head.

To the Downhill Skier

That cross-country skiing has long outlived its critics is no historical accident.

For starters, despite the electric thrill of Alpine skiing, the Nordic version has the advantage of being cheaper, more accessible, more sociable, better exercise, and certainly less crowded. Have you ever stood in a line to take off across a field or golf course for a morning cross-country run?

Not that this book intends to make a judgment of one over the other. Certainly, any skier who understands the heritage of the skimeister gives equal dignity to all forms of the sport. What is best about the ski age we live in is that we need not make choices about one over the other. The thrill of downhill skiing at high speed with those sure, crisp, steel-edged turns is undeniable. But if the last two decades have proved anything

in the entire world of skiing it is that Nordic, cross-country, ski touring, running—whatever term you use to identify the sport—is surely as exciting in its own right, and needn't be apologized for as "the alternative."

At the National Cross-Country Championships at Bretton Woods, New Hampshire in 1982, Tony asked Bill Koch, that year's World Cup winner, what seemed at the time an overly simplistic question: "What separates the winners from the near-winners in this sport of cross-country? Training, determination? The right wax?"

Koch thought for a moment, assessing his season, then answered in his characteristically humble way. "I've been doing well on the downhill sections," he said.

His coach, Mike Gallagher, explained more fully. All the skiers in the very top of a world class field are in peak condition. They've probably waxed the same, and surely all of them on that level are lion-hearted athletes. But Koch's success that year came from his greatness as a downhill skier. Touch, technique, the way he rode his skis so aggressively into turns,

15

flying downhill without the slightest tendency to hold back—it was the great downhiller in Koch that made the great skier and champion.

On the very next day, after the races, a gang of us went up to try the Bretton Woods NASTAR course on an Alpine slope. We were on Alpine skis. The clear winner among us through 25 slalom gates was Craig Ward, a member of the U.S. Nordic team who did the course on cross-country skis. And his were not the steel-edged, fatter compromise called a Norpine ski, either. Ward had skied the course on his light, stiff racing skis that usually require an act of God for us ordinary skiers to turn.

The point is that skiing is skiing is skiing. The division one supposes to exist between Nordic and Alpine forms is at best a thin cultural bias carried on by crabby folks who don't really understand skiing in its broadest sense.

We are in an age of such increasing expense in Alpine skiing that mixing the forms up is becoming ever more popular for the weekend ski family. It's a natural: A day of downhill, a day of cross-country. Actually, the other way around is probably better, since Saturdays are usually more crowded at Alpine areas than are Sundays.

What most downhill skiers find is that, rather than a cheap pastime as an alternative, Nordic is a workout that requires the same principles of balance, counter-rotation of the body, leaning well out over the skis, knees bent in the weight transfer of a Telemark turn. And beyond mere technical differences, Nordic skiing has its own rhythm and beauty, a kind of pendular symmetry the Alpine aficionado finds hauntingly familiar.

Several of the Nordic centers described in this book are combined with Alpine areas. From Stowe in Vermont to Waterville Valley, New Hampshire, to Kingfield, Maine, and the Sugarloaf environs, to Berkshire East in Massachusetts— wherever you find Alpine skiing there are bound to be some Nordic tracks nearby.

And so here is an invitation to any downhiller who one day feels just a bit down in the checkbook, who dreads another half-hour liftline, who is sick of fussing with 40 pounds of gear, who cannot bear one more chairlift ride of sub-arctic wind-chills, and who just may long for a day of utter solitude in the winter woods of New England: give Nordic a try. You can rent gear and buy trail maps, lunch, and a starter lesson all for about the price of a lift ticket. And you just might gain some skills that will make you a better downhiller.

Come on and give it a try. What do you have to lose but your prejudices?

Beyond the Good News

If there is a religious zeal among some cross-country skiers—and we're sure there is—then get ready for the real good news about the sport. We've always known cross-country skiing is good for body as well as soul. But how good?

Rising head and shoulders above the current wave of fitness gurus (despite her rather diminutive stature) is Jackie Sorenson, who did as much as anyone to popularize aerobic conditioning. Sorenson's facts have never been in question. Here is her latest calorie line on various physical regimens. If you're a 125-pound person (extrapolate for your weight) then 30 minutes of moderate walking will burn about 125 calories. If you can swim 30 yards per minute, you'll burn 175 calories in that same half hour; ditto for ice-skating.

Golf will take care of 160 calories per half hour, and moderate biking will burn 175, too, though strenuous biking will take care of 275. Now hiking: 185 calories per half hour. Good fast walking: 230. Into the rough stuff. Racquetball: 350 per half hour, with running pushing close to that figure, depending on how hard you pump the legs, of course.

We're sure you've guessed what's on the very top of this list. The heaviest calorie-burning sport of them all is that four-legged running routine called cross-country skiing. Per half hour, for a 125-pound person (a little person, really) the burn is 500 calories, with the effect all aerobic athletes know well—a high-calorie burn for up to four hours after the activity has stopped.

The explanation: Legs contain the vast bulk of muscle in the human and so the most energy is spent in vigorously exercising them. Now add to the legs, the next-largest groups—shoulders, chest, and arm muscles. Get them all working simultaneously and you have the highest calorie-burner of all, cross-country skiing. It's a little like running on all fours.

Off to the Races

As we explored earlier, cross-country skiing appeals on many levels. When Bill Koch won the 1982 World Cup, followed not far behind by such bright lights as Tim and Jennifer Caldwell, Dan Simoneau and others, it seemed that a top-flight ski racing tradition had finally taken root in America. Subsequent years proved that our early optimism was just that, and that the United States is still perhaps five or six generations behind the Europeans, Swedes and Finns most notably.

Yet the Koch years did much for the sport as a sport, the competitive level beyond recreational cruising. Among other things, they raised the consciousness of recreational skiers that, as in running, anyone who can ski can race. And anyone and everyone can ski.

So at one end of the sport is the purely leisure-oriented, relaxed recreationalist. His love is moving slowly through the winter snows and taking his time with his surroundings. That is the skiing most people understood up until the late 1970s when, for a lack of a better term, the Koch years were upon us. Racers, we learned, did not come out of some special School for the Very Hot. Indeed, most fast skiers were skiers who skied a lot, got in shape, and knew the discipline.

Again, as with running, though not everyone is blessed with equal talents, anyone can get in shape and learn to ski well enough to race. And this is the marvelous prospect of citizen ski racing: it is there for anyone who wants it.

Along the Ellis River Trail in the Jackson, New Hampshire, system there is a measured 200-meter section for skiers to time themselves. Tony once waited near the end of that stretch to watch how many skiers were actually working on their times. On this intermediate-level trail, out of a dozen skiers there were ten who ran across the line huffing and puffing and looking at their watches.

Call it the American way, call it competitive instinct, or just allow that there is a natural delight in going fast on skis, whatever, most skiers would love to race if they could. It is

just human nature, once we rise to a certain level of proficiency, to want to test ourselves against a standard. Almost all the major ski-touring centers have citizen races that can be entered for a fee of about a buck. On one level these races are merely fun, on another level they elevate the sport of cross-country skiing to an unimaginable height.

Yes, citizen racing has become equivalent to road-running races, and there are several important analogies. Foremost, to beat a point into the ground, is this: Racing is for everyone and anyone. The hot shots go out and duel for the top one-hundred spots, while the duffer may just like rounding the course to stop at the feed stations. Most skiers are somewhere in the middle. Their contest is against the course, and they're in quest of that old Personal Best.

Races vary from 2-kilometer sprints to 50-kilometer marathons. Nearly all of them are open registration. The United States Ski Association (USSA) has several race series across the country, from 10-kilometer runs to the Great America Ski Chase Series. This is a series of 8 marathons, one of which is held at Bretton Woods, New Hampshire, each year. (If marathon distance scares you, there is a one-loop, 25-kilometer version as well.)

One of the really fun races around is the annual Stowe Derby. Here, skiers take off from the top of Mount Mansfield, descend the fire trail for about two thousand feet (a shallow descent, really) then run the rest of the ten miles into the town of Stowe, Vermont. Like most citizen races, this is low-key. Many skiers make the run for the wonderful social climate before and during the race, and the beer blast afterward.

Aside from ordinary citizen touring, there are all kinds of kinky variations, such as Telemark races, downhill competitions dedicated to that artistic turn invented a century ago by Sondre Nordheim.

Then there is ski orienteering (Ski-O), a race through the wilderness in which skiers must also navigate with a compass and topographical map to find the course. This skiing dates to ancient military skills. Messengers from the Swedish or Finnish armies would have to find their way across the tundra to deliver crucial information. Thus performance skiing and woodsmanship were equally tested here, for going fast meant little in the wilderness if the messenger didn't know where he was going.

Then there's biathlon, triathlon, Nordic combined, and jumping—though these are rather specialized skills for the average weekend skier. Nevertheless, competition abounds everywhere, and on every level of seriousness. Nearly every large area has a school with all the information you'll need for the current season in this region. Or, simply ask at the desk of an area where you're skiing. Most likely there will be notices posted about upcoming citizen events.

If improvement is one of your skiing goals, regardless of your current level, there is perhaps no faster path to better performance than learning the disciplines of competitive skiing.

And doesn't that cold drink taste good after a race!

That Question: Wax

To start with an answer, I use both myself. How's that for a hedge?

The question: Who should use a no-wax ski, and who should wax?

I have heard so many sermons on this subject from so many sources that I am often reminded of two political parties in a campaign. Or two fishermen talking about the right fly to use in a stream.

I am also reminded of a heavy-bicycle/light-bicycle analogy. A fellow who runs a nearby bike shop was trying to sell a lightweight French racing bike to a customer who had come into the shop with his sights quite a bit lower. The customer asked what the French racing bike (at nearly twice the money) would do for him that the plainer, cheaper, heavier bike would not do.

"You can't even compare them," said the bike dealer. "It's just another level of the sport. The XYZ bike is more responsive and much much faster. It's another world."

Aside from the fact that the bike salesman had said nothing to really enlighten this customer, he left himself wide open, and had utterly no response to the buyer's powerful truth:

"I'm interested in exercise and riding with my family on vacation," said the fellow. "What does it matter how fast I can go?"

If this describes exactly your attitude toward cross-country skiing, as I know it does for many, then go with the no-wax or waxless skis. (Then put a thin protective coat of glider wax on them, anyway.)

Here are some other checkpoints for those who should probably go waxless:

. . . If you're an infrequent skier, half-a-dozen days or less on an average winter.

. . . If it drives you mad to slip backward, even a little bit, going uphill. And you hate to herringbone.

. . . If you live (and ski) in a part of the world where snow conditions vary greatly.

. . . If you hate equipment maintenance of all kinds, and waxing skis looks fussy, scary, and/or stupid.

. . . If the thing you like best about jogging is the simplicity of putting on the shoes and walking out your door.

By these last checkpoints, do not get the idea that waxing is an overly laborious or time-consuming job. I know one certified teacher who goes for an hour's ski run every morning before teaching. His waxing method is to look at the thermometer, and then to spend less than five minutes waxing his skis before his run. It is his well-founded belief that if being off by a color really jiggles a skier unless he is racing, then there's something wrong in his technique.

But back to the waxless skier. As I say, I use both. My waxless skis are mid-thickness Trak Pacers. They are not light weight, nor are they heavy trucks. The ridge-pattern that gives them grip runs over a kick zone of moderate length. In other words, these are mid-everything skis. They'd be right for everyone except the competition skier, or that highly experienced runner who likes the feel of flying with wings on his feet.

Much of my casual cross-country skiing begins at my back door. I'll get an hour or more daily when the snow is good. I ski for a couple of miles through unpathed, hilly woods, ducking through occasional underbrush, then I emerge on a bridle path that circles a horse farm, cross through a broad tree farm beside it, running down through rows of evergreens that make me feel a little like a rat in a maze. Then I pop clear on a lovely 18-hole golf course, of which I can digest as much or as little as I have time for before I plunge back into the woods for the trek home.

If the snow is new and deep, I will most likely take the waxless skis. Their size and weight make them easier to break trail with and I'm not so likely to break one on the jagged woods floor. Though I'm interested, from an exercise point of view, in keeping a good aerobic pace going, speed per se is not my goal in such conditions. Waxless skis are the choice.

But there is another sort of day. The snow has settled and "set up." In the previous days I have skied tracks into my course, and it may even be a bit firm and fast today. I am not planning any exploration forays off through unfamiliar woods, and I have a notion to run a few miles—that is, to ski as fast a pace as I can, to get a nice rhythmic diagonal stride going, to huff and puff a bit.

Or I am at a touring center with trails groomed and track-set. Again, my purpose is to work out, to ski fast and steadily for at least half an hour before a break. In these latter instances, I'll use my pair of skinny, very light and stiff Jarvinen racing skis. Exactly why, when I'm not in a competition of any kind, is hard to say, but it comes down to a matter of feel. The light skinny skis—waxed close to correctly so you're not slipping backward or picking up balls of snow on the kick zone—somehow encourages the skier to go at it a bit more intensely. He leans out over the skis more, throws his hip more into the stride, the pole hand reaching further out and up as he settles into that nice easy rhythm that looks nearly effortless though it produces maximum speed.

Of course the same pleasing rhythm of the diagonal stride can be performed on waxless skis as well. But the lightweight waxed ski heightens that pleasure to the extreme. The feet feel nearly weightless as the skis glide faster and faster over the snow, and now the skier is into that often-overlooked element in cross-country skiing—speed. And speed on skis reads fun.

This is not to suggest that everyone go buy two pair of skis simply to explore the extreme range of the sport. But for someone who plans to spend plenty of winter hours working out on skis in the way described above—skiing tracks and predictable terrain—and who finds the prospect of messing around with waxes sort of fun, or at least not disagreeable, then a pair of waxable skis may be in order.

As I said at the outset, this is a rather hedged answer. I own two pairs of skis to prove it.

If you have skied several times on your waxless skis, and want to feel the difference, try a demo. Most of the larger touring centers will have most varieties of skis on hand. And if it is clear you are taking a demo run, many rental shops will wax the skis for you and give you a complimentary hour on them. This may also be a good time for some instruction, for lightweight waxed skis are not quite as forgiving of sloppy technique as are most waxless skis.

Waxing Up

So you do go with a pair of waxable skis: now what about the waxing?

I do not suppose there is any more-discussed issue in the sport than waxing. It seems to come down to equal parts knowledge, instinct, application technique, and magic.

In the Sierra Nevadas in the 1850s, when mining camps placed heavy wagers of gold dust on miners who would represent them in ski races, the contest often came down to the "doper." He was the ski preparer. In utter secrecy the night before the race, he would mix up his special potion of beeswax, paraffin, and whatever other hopefully charmed ingredients he could think of to apply to the ski bottoms. So much money rode on these races that the doper was regarded as something like the witch doctor who could conjure up just the right spell to make the bottoms of a pair of skis fast.

I am not sure anyone really knows how wax works, though I have listened to many hours of theory. The most cogent primer I recall was that of Jack Turner, a member of the U.S. Ski Team, who at breakfast one morning explained as he diagrammed on his napkin, the following:

Crystals of snow come hard-edged, as in a new snowfall in cold weather, or the smooth-sided crystal of snow that has thawed and refrozen a few times.

24

The wax of the day must be sufficiently soft so the crystals of snow will penetrate enough to give the ski its grip, but not penetrate so completely that snow will stick to the ski. If the wax you choose for the day is too hard, there will be so little penetration of crystals into the wax, that the ski will slip backward when you try to push off on it. Sometimes, good ski technique can get around this tendency, if the problem isn't too extreme. But in the opposite case, the wax is so soft, the penetration of snow crystals so extreme, the skier will pick up great immobilizing clumps of snow on the kick zone of the ski.

Look elsewhere for a detailed explanation of ski waxing in all its nuance. There are several excellent books on the market, and many of the larger areas will even put on waxing clinics from time to time. Moreover, the more days you ski with people who know what they're about, the quicker you will learn for yourself. And, when all else fails, when you want to know the wax of the day, ask a hot shot. At every touring center I've been to, the morning air is full of discussion about the wax of the day. Listen to this talk. You'll know who the hot shots are right away.

That said, here is the Chamberlain Sometimes Sure-Fire Simpleminded Waxing Style:

Cross-country waxes are color-coded to temperature, and are pretty logical about it. Cold colors—blue and green—are cold temperature waxes, and warm colors—purples to reds—are for warmer temperatures. So you stick a thermometer in the snow and know just what to do, correct? For real arctic snow, green will be the choice (or maybe special green), blue for merely cold snow, violet for that 32-degree Fahrenheit limbo, and red for thawing snow.

Well, it's almost that simple. But not really.

Despite the temperature, if your snow has thawed and refrozen, its crystal shape will have changed irreversibly. Yesterday's hard-edged new snow, having thawed once or twice, has now lost those hard crystal edges and become old snow with round crystals. Often, the only way to get a grip on such crystals is by using klister, gooey stuff that comes in tubes and is color-coded similarly to the hard waxes.

Swix is not the only wax manufacturer around, but it is certainly an identifiable standard. There is a Swix kit that comes complete with all the waxes and klisters you will need. Armed with this kit, a scraper, polishing cork, a rag or paper toweling and a lightweight propane torch, you must answer two questions: What is the temperature of the snow? Are the crystals sharp (newer) or rounded (old)?

If you're a real performance skier, you'll put a grip wax (softer) on the kick zone, and a glider (harder) wax on tips and tails. But that's pretty fussy and unnecessary for most users of fiberglass skis. Most of us will put a glider wax—green is my choice—over the entire base of the ski. This seals the bottom, protects it, and is a good base to apply the wax of the day over. In many cases this base wax is applied just at the beginning of the season. After rubbing on the wax, heat it gently with the torch, then polish it in to a slick finish. (You may also make this application with a cool iron , the same as with Alpine skis, and cork-polish.)

Over this base coat (which you probably have prepared at home) you'll then make your best guess at the wax of the day. Even the neophyte, if he has listened to those around him, can come close. Read the wax tube for temperature range, look at your thermometer. If it's fluffy stuff, go green. If it crunches a bit, blue. If it's good packing for snowballs, purple. If it's mashed potatoes, red. And if you're very, very lucky, you can skip the klister; at any rate, start without it.

Also keep in mind:

. . . As a general rule, go with the colder wax. Snow temperature is generally far behind the temperature of a warming day, and the penalty for being too cold is not so great as the other way around. Wax too warm, and you'll be planted like a statue. Also, you can apply warm wax over cold, and klister over hard wax, but it is almost impossible to do the reverse.

. . . We New Englanders must also watch humidity. On very humid days, it often pays to wax warmer than temperature indicates.

. . . If you're on prepared tracks you can wax warmer, get more kick without paying the price of clinging clumps. But in unbroken snow when bushwhacking woods and mountain terrain, wax colder.

You are supposed to do all this waxing in a warm room, either at home, or a waxing room at a touring center, with the skis at room temperature. But I've seen plenty of top-flight ski racers sitting on the bumpers of their cars waxing before a race. Skiers often must wax while under way on the trail, too.

Most fiberglass skis have kick zones well-marked, but a rule of thumb is to wax from about one foot in front of the bindings to one foot behind. Rub the wax on side-to-side in overlapping smears. Then take your cork and rub it over the wax fast enough to let friction soften it to a nice polish. Repeat this waxing procedure twice, and you're set for the day, unless you must rewax for changing conditions.

Suppose you've blown it? You get out on the trail, and you've got big balls of snow under your feet? And everyone says you can't wax down in color?

Here is where you'll learn fast that, like fly fishing and choosing the right pattern for a salmon stream, no rules are cast in concrete about ski waxing. Get out the scraper and do the best you can to get the wrong wax off, then try to smear the colder wax on. If it doesn't work, daub some cold klister over the whole mess and see if that helps.

There are difficult days for waxing, right around freezing. The best rule I have discovered about these days is to stay on flat terrain. Remember, the worst that can happen is you'll end up walking back to bloody mary hour with the skis on your shoulder.

What to Wear

Dressing for cross-country is a difficult but soluble problem. The key is layers.

Layers of thin clothing can be taken off as the skier heats up, then put back on when he stops pumping and begins to cool down. A typical outfit for a typical day: polypropylene underwear (use nothing else), wind pants below, a light jersey, loose shirt, light sweater, and a nylon shell. Although knickers and Nordic snowflake stockings look natty at the touring center, wear nylon gaiters in the back country. These in effect extend the waterproof seal of your ski boots up nearly to the knees.

There are all kinds of clothing variations, of course, and if you're really trekking in backcountry, you'll want to pack clothes in which you could survive a winter night.

This goes for the minimal tools, too: screwdriver and duct tape, wax, sunglasses, Chapstick, matches, a compass, topographic maps, and any other miscellany you may need on the trail. But keep it simple. Camping stoves and elaborate waxing kits are examples of the unnecessary for me. They don't feel heavy until the tenth mile or so.

CONNECTICUT

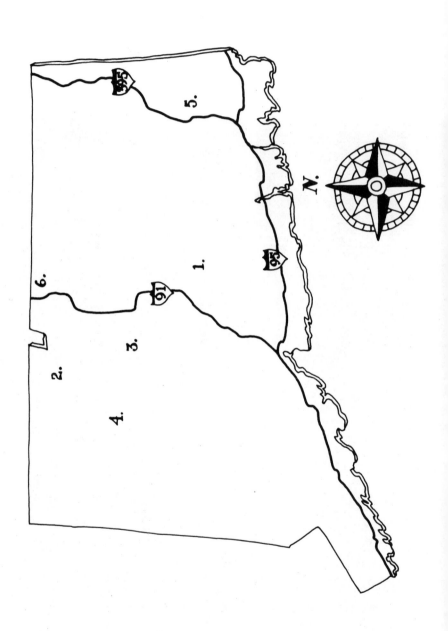

Connecticut

Numbers on map refer to towns numbered below

SKUNGAMAUG CLUBS
Folly Lane
Coventry, Connecticut 06238
203-742-9348

Hours: 9 a.m. to dusk.
Trail System: 12 kilometers (about 7 miles).
Trail Difficulty: Easiest, more difficult.
Trail Grooming: Groomed and trackset as needed.
Rental Equipment: 30 sets.
Instruction: PSIA-certified.
Food Facilities: Snack bar serves hot and cold drinks, sand-wiches.
Lodging: Motel 10 miles distant.
How to Get There: I-84 to Exit 99; south on Route 195 to Goose Lane; turn right and follow to stop sign, then bear right onto a dirt road and the touring center.

This is classic golf course skiing, with most trails cut over gently rolling terrain that doesn't pose much challenge unless you want to get athletic about things. There is one loop that leads through woods, and as skiers roll along, they will pass ponds with ice skaters. Though the trail system is limited in size and variation, there still seems to be plenty of skiing here through a pretty picture of winter.

PINE MOUNTAIN SKI TOURING CENTER
Route 179
East Hartland, Connecticut 06027
203-653-4279

Hours: 8:30 a.m. to dusk.
Trail System: About 28 kilometers (20 miles).
Trail Difficulty: Easiest, more difficult, most difficult.
Trail Grooming: Groomed and trackset.
Rental Equipment: 220 sets.
Instruction: By appointment.
Food Facilities: Snack bar at the center; restaurants nearby.

Lodging: Several inns and motels in the area.

How to Get There: Massachusetts Turnpike to I-91 south of Bradley Field at Exit 40; Route 20 west through East Granby, Granby, and East Hartland, Connecticut; Route 179 south for 2 miles to Pine Mountain.

Even when it rains in much of southern New England, Pine Mountain, the state's second-highest peak at 1,300 feet, usually has a snow covering. The area, located in grand rural snow country about 25 miles northwest from Hartford, features nicely groomed trails through woods and open meadows. While much of this skiing is fast and flat, there are some jerky twisting trails that challenge your skiing skills as well. The center has a full complement of rentals and retail gear, and lunch tables and booths around a huge woodstove. Several motels and inns can be found nearby, including the famous Yankee Peddler Inn and The Old Riverton Inn.

WINDING TRAILS SKI TOURING CENTER
Off Route 4
Farmington, Connecticut 06032
203-677-8458

Hours: 9 a.m. to 4:30 p.m.

Trail System: 26 kilometers (about 15 miles).

Trail Difficulty: Easiest, more difficult.

Trail Grooming: Machine groomed (about 8 percent) with the rest skier-tracked.

Rental Equipment: About 200 sets.

Instruction: Group and private.

Food Facilities: Snack bar.

Lodging: Several inns and motels in the area.

How to Get There: I-84 to Exit 39, then 1 mile west of Farmington Center to the Winding Trails Farm.

Winding Trails is a 400-acre touring center set in the picturesque hills of the Connecticut countryside. The entire trail system—a relatively gentle series of loops over open pasture and wooded roads—is groomed carefully and trackset for smooth, fast skiing. This is an excellent course for the runners of the sport. The center itself has a well-stocked rental shop and places heavy emphasis on its instructional program. Winding Trails is open December through March, during which it throws six nightly wine and cheese parties after a moonlight ski tour. In mid-January the center stages its annual Citizen's Race.

THE WHITE MEMORIAL FOUNDATION
Route 202; Box 368
Litchfield, Connecticut 06759
203-567-0857

Hours: Tuesday through Saturday, 8:30 a.m. to 4:30 p.m.; Sunday 2 p.m. to 5 p.m.
Trail System: 48 kilometers (about 30 miles).
Trail Difficulty: Easiest, more difficult, most difficult.
Trail Grooming: None.
Rental Equipment: At the Wilderness Shop in Litchfield.
Instruction: No.
Food Facilities: In Litchfield.
Lodging: Inns and motels in the area.
How to Get There: From Hartford, Route 202 west through Litchfield for 2½ miles to a left turn at the White Memorial sign.

The White Memorial Foundation is a lovely 4000-acre sanctuary dedicated to conservation, education, recreation, and nature research. The terrain, with its criss-crossing carriage roads and trails, is still in its uninterrupted natural state; no motor vehicles are allowed anywhere on the property. The skiing is of the primitive, bushwhacking variety, though tracks are generally cut by previous skiers. The countryside is not especially challenging, except to runners, though one or two real twisters can be found if someone really wants to find them. The trail loops roll through woods down to the shores of

Bantam Lake. There is no trail fee here, though maps may be purchased at the museum for about $1. A warming-waxing-picnicking facility is also available.

QUINEBAUG VALLEY SKI TOURING CENTER
Roosevelt Avenue, Box 29
Norwich, Connecticut 06360
203-886-2284

Hours: 9 a.m. to 4 p.m.
Trail System: 11 kilometers (about 7 miles).
Trail Difficulty: Easiest, more difficult, most difficult.
Trail Grooming: Packed but not trackset.
Rental Equipment: 100 sets.
Instruction: PSIA-certified instructor on weekends.
Food Facilities: Snack bar at the center.
Lodging: Hotels, inns, and motels 3 miles distant.
How to Get There: Connecticut Turnpike to Route 12 in Norwich. Follow signs.

This active dairy farm features that most pleasant sort of open-field skiing that lets the inexperienced skier practice in a low-stress environment, but also allows runners to really work out over tracks well set by previous skiers. From the open fields—cow pastures—skiers can access the nearby woodlands that glance in and out of open pastures. This is fine touring when the snow is available. Norwich is a good-sized town just three miles from the touring center, and has an entire range of rentals, retail, food, and lodging.

CEDAR BROOK FARMS SKI TOURING CENTER
1481 Ratley Road
West Suffield, Connecticut 06093
203-668-5026

Hours: 9 a.m. to dusk
Trail System: 10 kilometers (6.2 miles).
Trail Difficulty: Easiest, more difficult.

Trail Grooming: Groomed and trackset.
Rental Equipment: 300 sets.
Instruction: Yes.
Food Facilities: Small snack bar for soups and sandwiches.
Lodging: In the area.
How to Get There: Massachusetts Turnpike to Hartford; I-91 to
   Route 57 through Feeding Hills to Ratley Road on left.

When the snow is right, this 200-acre touring center has all the delights of skiing on a real working New England farm with pastureland, woods, ponds, and streams well within the reach of all skiers. Animals (safely confined) watch as you pass through the pasture. From this open skiing, the trails course through a very pretty woodland area, then bring skiers back into the pasture. This can be hard-run ski touring, or pleasant, gentle cruising, as you wish. There's a warming hut on the property as skiers cross over for a loop through Enchanted Forest, and back through Cornstalk Patch and Scarecrow Hill. Fanciful names, delightful skiing.

MASSACHUSETTS

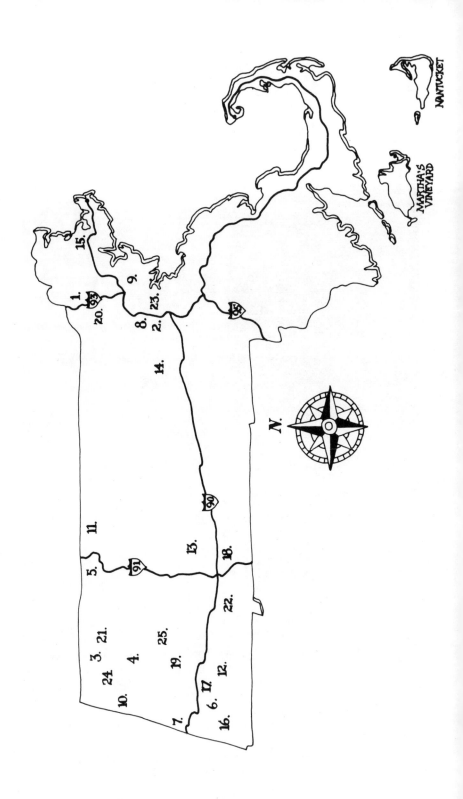

Massachusetts

Numbers on map refer to towns numbered below

ROLLING GREEN
311 Lowell Street
Andover, Massachusetts 01810
617-475-4066

Hours: 9 a.m. to 4:30 p.m.; night skiing 6 to 9, Tuesday to
    Friday.
Trail System: 5 kilometers (about 3 miles).
Trail Difficulty: Easiest, more difficult.
Trail Grooming: As needed.
Rental Equipment: 100 sets.
Instruction: PSIA-certified.
Food Facilities: Trail snacks at the center; also a lounge.
Lodging: Sheraton Rolling Green Hotel.
How to Get There: Route 93 to Massachusetts Exit 17; Shera-
    ton is on the right. Touring Center is at the Rolling Green
    Hotel.

Rolling Green is a convenient touring area near downtown
Boston, yet is surprisingly pleasant skiing with a nice feel of
terrain to it. Not upcountry wilderness skiing to be sure, still a
fine place to get in shape for those trips, a good midday workout spot, and some real fun and exercise for city people who
have only evening hours for themselves. A full weekend lighted
loop lets you take those 2-hour vacations that make the next
day possible. This is also tied into a major hotel with all the
amenities.

GREAT BROOK FARM SKI TOURING CENTER
96 Pleasant Hill Lane
Carlisle, Massachusetts 01741
617-369-7486

Hours: 9 a.m. to 4:30 p.m.; Tuesday and Thursday, 9 a.m. to 9
    p.m.
Trail System: 15 kilometers (about 9 miles).
Trail Difficulty: Easiest, more difficult, most difficult.
Trail Grooming: Groomed and double trackset.

Rental Equipment: Yes.
Instruction: Certified professional ski school.
Food Facilities: Snacks, hot cider, coffee, tea.
Lodging: None.
How to Get There: I-495 to Route 4 in Chelmsford; right on Route 4 and follow to Lowell Road.

Just 40 minutes from Boston, Great Brook Farm is a fine and complete daytrip ski center with its 15-kilometer trail system winding over farm meadows, through deep woodlands, and over frozen ponds. Like the Weston Track, Great Brook is one of very few areas that offers snowmaking over a 1-kilometer loop. Night skiing is also available over a 1.5-kilometer loop.

Great Brook caters to organized race programs, youth groups, and puts on a citizen's race every Tuesday night. There is an organized Bill Koch League for grade-schoolers.

The area is perfect for Boston-area recreational skiers looking for regular exercising, or to get in shape for upcountry.

NORTH COUNTRY SKI TOURING CENTER

Carlisle State Forest, Lowell Road
Carlisle, Massachusetts 01741
617-369-7486

Hours: 9 a.m. to 4:30 p.m.; Tuesday and Thursday night skiing until 9.
Trail System: 18 kilometers (about 10 miles).
Trail Difficulty: Easiest, more difficult.
Trail Grooming: Yes.
Rental Equipment: Yes.
Instruction: PSIA-certified.
Food Facilities: Snack bar at the Hart Barn.
Lodging: Hotels and motels in the region.
How to Get There: I-495 to Route 225 east to Carlisle, then north on Lowell Road.

This is another area with the nicely civilized feel of Boston about it. The touring is excellent, encompassing about 500 acres of terrain from cruising golf course trails to bushwhacking thicket. Much of the touring is over old roads, so the remaining trails are comfortably wide—just in case you have forgotten what it's like to ski beside your spouse rather than behind. There are Tuesday night races across a 1.3 kilometer loop of manmade snow. The Hart Barn is the heart of the center. Its woodstoves sear with heat all winter as skiers get study maps, wax their bottoms, or just rest their weary bones as they sip hot chocolate. Trail snacks are available from the center, as well as some instruction.

BERKSHIRE EAST
South River Road
Charlemont, Massachusetts 01339
413-339-6617

Hours: 9 a.m. to 4:30 p.m.
Trail System: 7 kilometers (about 4 miles).
Trail Difficulty: Easiest, more difficult, most difficult.
Trail Grooming: No.
Rental Equipment: No.
Instruction: No.
Food Facilities: Two lodges in the area serve full meals.
Lodging: Motels and inns in the area.
How to Get There: Route 2 to Charlemont to South River Road;
    signs to Berkshire East.

This small touring area makes use of the fine Alpine skiing at Berkshire East. It is a fine place to practice Telemark artistry, and the downhill area provides the basic creature comforts: warmth and food. The trails are in the pretty Berkshire foothill country, with thick spruce forest and gentle fields that are usually tracked by skiers ahead. There is wilderness bushwhacking here as well, over varied terrain.

CUMMINGTON FARM CROSS-COUNTRY SKI RESORT
South Road
Cummington, Massachusetts 01026
413-634-2111

Hours: 9 a.m. to 5 p.m.; Thursday through Saturday evenings, 7 to 10 p.m.
Trail System: 42 kilometers with 2 kilometers lighted for night skiing.
Trail Difficulty: Easiest (most), more difficult, most difficult.
Trail Grooming: As needed. Machine trackset.
Rental Equipment: 300 sets.
Instruction: PSIA-certified school.
Food Facilities: Restaurant at resort.
Lodging: 10 rustic cabins on ski trails; Old Sugar House dormitory.
How to Get There: Massachusetts Turnpike to Route 91 north to Northampton; Route 9 west to Cummington (26 miles); turn right into town and follow signs.

Cummington Farm, at 1,400 feet in the Berkshire uplands, is the largest and among the most-popular ski-touring areas in southern New England. With the good elevation despite the southerly location, the skiing usually remains long into the spring. Ski touring is the sole business of Cummington Farm, and it shows in the experience the farm offers.

The well-marked and groomed trail system is spread out over 700 acres of rolling foothills that take skiers through the hardwood forests of the wild turkey, and over dazzling white meadowland. The trail difficulty is geared toward novice and intermediate skiers with a nice, leisurely "low-stress" feel about the place. Still, citizen racing, including one of the country's largest—Cummington Farm Bread Race (early March)—and moonlight tours, are common here as well.

The accommodations include a wonderfully big restaurant, dormitory lodging, as well as a package with two meals, skiing, and a night in one of the woodstove-heated log cabins. There is a well-appointed Nordic retail store as well.

OAK RIDGE SKI TOURING CENTER
Oak Ridge Golf Club
West Gill Road
Gill, Massachusetts 01376
413-863-9693

Hours: Daily except Monday 8 a.m. to dusk. Tobagganing at
    night.
Trail System: 16 kilometers (about 10 miles).
Trail Difficulty: Easiest, more difficult. Beginners area.
Trail Grooming: Daily.
Rental Equipment: Yes.
Instruction: Weekends.
Food Facilities: Sandwiches, hot soups, stews; full bar and
    fireplaced lounge.
Lodging: Nearby.
How to Get There: I-91 to Route 2; east to Exit 27. Take Main
    Road to West Gill Road.

The Oak Ridge center is an excellent example of golf-course
skiing. The same picturesque setting that pleases golfers in
the summer is there for skiers on 100 acres of gently-rolling
meadowland and silent hardwood thickets. The trails are carefully groomed and trackset; there is open field skiing as well.
Oak Ridge offers PSIA instruction and guided tours, and
moonlight excursions. The lodge features food and drink
around a big fire.

BUTTERNUT SKI TOURING
Route 23 (Butternut Ski Area Access Road)
Great Barrington, Massachusetts 01230
413-528-0610

Hours: 9 a.m. to 4 p.m. Thursday through Sunday and school
    vacation weeks.
Trail System: 7 kilometers of tracks, plus open field skiing.
Trail Difficulty: Easiest, more difficult.
Trail Grooming: Daily.

Rental Equipment: 100 sets.
Instruction: PSIA-certified; group and private lessons.
Food Facilities: Cafeteria at the Butternut Ski Area.
Lodging: Inns, motels, and guest houses in the area.
How to Get There: I-90 to Exit 2 at Lee, Massachusetts; Route
     102 west to Route 7 south to Route 23, then east to Butter-
     nut.

Like many touring areas associated with established downhill
areas, Butternut Ski Touring shares the benefits of the Alpine
accommodations (including the nursery for three- to six-year-
olds), and naturally lures the skinny skiers onto the Alpine
slopes to take a shot at some Telemarking. Whether there is
any truth to the old chestnut, "If you can walk, you can cross-
country ski," it definitely does not apply to Telemark turning
on downhill slopes. Butternut, however, is an excellent place
to get lessons for this graceful move. The area has an excellent
ski school that can take you to the downhill slopes for lessons.

     Spreading out from the warming hut beside a pretty
pond, the touring area is a pristine piece of the Berkshire
countryside whose 7 miles of gentle, well-groomed trails lead
into a 45-kilometer trail system in the nearby Beartown State
Forest; the touring center has maps of this system.

KENNEDY PARK
Lenox, Massachusetts 01240
413-637-3010

Hours: 7 a.m. to 4 p.m.
Trail System: None; 600-acre park.
Trail Difficulty: Easiest, more difficult.
Trail Grooming: No.
Rental Equipment: At a nearby ski shop. Call for details.
Instruction: No.
Food Facilities: In the Lenox area.
Lodging: In the area.
How to Get There: Take Massachusetts Turnpike to Exit 2; west
     on Route 7 then south to the park in Lenox.

Kennedy Park is an open 600-acre recreation area used year-round for a variety of sports. There is some gladed and wooded terrain around the park, and the number of skiers who use the land make good tracks for those who do not like breaking trail. While there are no facilities at the park itself, this Berkshire town offers all services, from food to rentals and retail facilities.

PLEASANT VALLEY
472 West Mountain Road
Lenox, Massachusetts 01240
413-637-0320

Hours: 9 a.m. to 5 p.m.
Trail System: 8 kilometers (about 4 miles).
Trail Difficulty: Easiest, more difficult.
Trail Grooming: None.
Rental Equipment: None at the area, but rental shop nearby.
Instruction: Some classes and workshops available to pre-registering skiers.
Food Facilities: In the Lenox area.
Lodging: In the area.
How to Get There: Massachusetts Turnpike to Lenox Exit; Route 7 to the intersection at Route 20 in Lenox; north for 3 miles to West Dugway Road; left for 1.6 miles to the sanctuary entrance.

Like Canoe Meadows, Pleasant Valley is a piece of open wildland owned by the Massachusetts Audubon Society and maintained as a wildlife sanctuary. It is a lovely 730-acre tract of semi-forested land that features beaver ponds, meadows, and hemlock gorge. Though the 7 miles of hiking trails are not groomed or trackset for skiing, only the most pettish would be troubled. It is a perfect serene area for the daytrip or the picnicking skier.

THE RESORT AT FOXHOLLOW
Route 7
Lenox, Massachusetts 01240
413-637-2000

Hours: 9 a.m. to 5 p.m.
Trail System: About 20 kilometers (14 miles).
Trail Difficulty: Easiest, more difficult, most difficult.
Trail Grooming: As needed.
Rental Equipment: Yes.
Instruction: Yes.
Food Facilities: Gourmet dining on premises (three-star Mobil rating).
Lodging: 34-room country inn (European plan), time-sharing condominium.
How to Get There: Massachusetts Turnpike to Exit 2; west on Route 20; Route 7 south to the resort in Lenox.

Foxhollow offers a fair-sized trail network that encompasses both the Berkshire hardwood forests and open meadowlands. Trails are well marked with standard Nordic signs, and the grooming is good over trails of all difficulty levels. Snowmobiles are not permitted on Foxhollow's trail network.

Rentals, maps, instruction, and guided tours are available, and the inn's lounge and dining facilities are open to day skiers as well as lodgers.

LINCOLN GUIDE SERVICE
Lincoln Road
Lincoln, Massachusetts 01773
617-259-9204

Hours: Monday through Wednesday 9 a.m. to 6 p.m.; Thursday and Friday 9 a.m. to 8 p.m.; Saturday and Sunday 9 a.m. to 5 p.m.

Trail System: 16 kilometers (about 10 miles).

Trail Difficulty: Easiest, more difficult.

Trail Grooming: None.

Rental Equipment: 200 sets.

Instruction: PSIA-certified.

Food Facilities: The nearest of three restaurants is within 50 yards of the skiing.

Lodging: Motels in the area.

How to Get There: I-95 to Exit 47 (Trapelo Road); west for 2 miles; left at the Lincoln Street stop sign, then 1 mile to the center.

Connected with the Weston Ski Track, Lincoln Guide Service is partly a retail operation that accesses town-owned conservation land, and partly a dream of Mike Farny to put together a significant touring area especially convenient to people from greater Boston. The open conservation land begins at the center's back door, and a rolling, well-groomed trail system branches out through the country where Henry David Thoreau hiked and observed nature. One of the trails, in fact, leads skiers along ponds of the Sudbury River to Thoreau's beloved Walden Pond in Concord, while other trails mix challenge with relaxing cruises. All trails are well-marked, and the center is well-stocked with rental and retail goods.

LYNN WOODS SKI TOURING CENTER
Route 129
Lynn, Massachusetts 01904
617-598-4212

Hours: 9 a.m. to dusk.
Trail System: 2200 acres with no set trails.
Trail Difficulty: Easiest, more difficult, most difficult.
Trail Grooming: No.
Rental Equipment: 150 sets.
Instruction: PSIA-certified.
Food Facilities: Snack bar at the center; full restaurants nearby.
Lodging: Motels nearby in the area.
How to Get There: I-95 to Route 129; southeast 2 miles to the Lynn Woods; the center is on the Gannon Municipal Golf Course.

Despite its closeness to Boston—just 20 minutes by car—the Lynn Woods is huge and woolly, encompassing a golf course, utility roads and woodlands, along with wild bushwhacking terrain. There are flats, cruising rollers, and some real hills here for every level skier. The center, a country clubhouse, has refreshments, plenty of waxing and relaxing room, snack bar, retail sales, and rentals. Instruction is available on weekends, and by appointment during the week. This is excellent ski touring within easy access of Boston.

BRODIE MOUNTAIN SKI RESORT
Route 7
New Ashford, Massachusetts 01237
413-443-4752

Hours: 9 a.m. to 5 p.m.
Trail System: 25 kilometers (about 16 miles).
Trail Difficulty: Easiest, more difficult, most difficult.
Trail Grooming: Yes.
Rental Equipment: Yes.
Instruction: Yes.
Food Facilities: The Blarney Room in the main lodge.
Lodging: Hotel at the ski area, and several facilities nearby.
How to Get There: Route 2 to Route 7; north for 9 miles beyond
    Pittsfield.

This popular Berkshire-region Alpine area incorporates the advantages of snow-making and baselodge facilities into its Nordic facility. The trail system combines about 15 kilometers of wide, groomed and trackset trails with another 25 miles of wilderness touring, then limitless bushwhacking out in the Mount Greylock Reservation. The skiing has good variety, from rolling pastureland and open fields, to heart-pumping hills and closed, wooded roads that meander through these Berkshire foothills, and past some most unusual rock formations. This is a land fecund with wildlife of all kinds. The groomed trail system was designed by former Olympic skier Bud Fischer and is used for training by the Williams College Ski Team. Night skiing is available, and several races are staged here throughout the season.

NORTHFIELD MOUNTAIN SKI TOURING CENTER
Route 63
Northfield, Massachusetts 01360
413-659-3713

Hours: 9 a.m. to 5 p.m.
Trail System: 40 kilometers (about 25 miles).
Trail Difficulty: Easiest, more difficult, most difficult.

Trail Grooming: Daily.
Rental Equipment: Yes.
Instruction: PSIA-certified.
Food Facilities: Chocolate Pot snack area; outdoor barbecue-pit food service at baselodge; both on weekends and holidays only.
Lodging: Several motels and inns within 5 miles of the center.
How to Get There: I-91 to Exit 27; Route 2 east to Route 63 north; 2 miles to the center.

More than 40 kilometers of double tracks set daily over wide trails groomed with Alpine equipment, an active racing program, and a lineup of instructors who teach some 5,000 skiers annually, make Northfield one of the largest learning centers in southern New England. The area pioneered the concept of grooming with Alpine rollers and prides itself on creating a ski surface just a little bigger and better than average.

In addition to recreational family touring, Northfield also takes pride in its Fast-Track Ski Camp for would-be racers who want to learn the sport from the likes of former U.S. Ski Team Olympian Tim Caldwell. Hank Lange and John Tidd are also PSIA-instructors.

Three well-traveled trail systems converge at The Chocolate Pot, where skiers warm themselves in front of a big fire and sip hot chocolate and soup. Other snacks are available from an outdoor barbecue pit. During the week Northfield Mountain offers instruction and rentals for elementary school-agers. Six miles of trails are reserved for snowshoers.

OTIS RIDGE TOURING CENTER
Box 128, Route 23
Otis, Massachusetts 01253
413-269-4444

Hours: 9 a.m. to 4 p.m.
Trail System: 38 kilometers (about 24 miles) in the state forest; 4 miles at the touring center.
Trail Difficulty: Easiest, more difficult, most difficult.

Trail Grooming: As needed, only at the touring center.
Rental Equipment: Yes.
Instruction: Yes.
Food Facilities: Grouse House Restaurant; cafeteria at the baselodge.
Lodging: 10 rooms at the Grouse House.
How to Get There: I-91 to West Springfield, Massachusetts; Route 20 west to Route 23; west to Otis Ridge; area is on the left shortly beyond the junction of Route 8.

Otis Ridge is a fine and popular Berkshire Alpine ski area that maintains 4 miles of nicely groomed touring trails on its back side. These gently rolling trails feed into the Otis State Forest system, a trail network of about 20 groomed miles that hit every level of difficulty and challenge. These trails include the famous Knox Trail, and several of the loops touch the Spectacle Ponds. There is nightlife to be had at the Grouse House, including a bar and restaurant. In January there is a Winter Carnival.

CANOE MEADOWS
Holmes Road
Pittsfield, Massachusetts 01201
413-637-0320

Hours: 9 a.m. to 5 p.m.
Trail System: 9 kilometers (about 5 miles).
Trail Difficulty: Easiest, more difficult.
Trail Grooming: No.
Rental Equipment: None at facility. Ski shop nearby.
Instruction: None.
Food Facilities: None at ski area, but restaurants nearby.
Lodging: Motels and inns in area.
How to Get There: Massachusetts Turnpike to Exit 2 at Lee; Route 7 to Holmes Road. Turn right and drive for 2 miles to entrance of Canoe Meadows Wildlife Sanctuary.

Canoe Meadows is a Massachusetts Audubon Society sanctuary comprised of 240 wooded acres bordered by the Housatonic River. It is not so much a ski facility as simply a lovely piece of wild land open for daily ski touring. There are tours of the property by appointment. An outhouse is available on the site.

WACHUSETT MOUNTAIN SKI AREA
Mountain Road
Princeton, Massachusetts 01541
617-464-5101

Hours: Weekdays 9 a.m. to dusk; Saturday, Sunday, and holidays, 8 a.m. to dusk.
Trail System: 25 kilometers (about 16 miles).
Trail Difficulty: Easiest, more difficult, most difficult.
Trail Grooming: 20 kilometers groomed and trackset.
Rental Equipment: 100 sets.
Instruction: 10:30 a.m. to 1 p.m., or by appointment. Telemark. PSIA instructors.
Food Facilities: Full cafeteria with lounge and ice cream shop.
Lodging: Several hotels and motels within a 15-minute drive.
How to Get There: Route 2 west to Route 140 south. The area is 3½ miles from the exit.

Close to Boston, Wachusett is another of those touring areas that brings the amenities of the downhill area, and the challenge to cross-country skiers to try their hand—and feet—at Telemarking down Alpine slopes. Instruction is necessary for this, and it is available. The area's 11 miles of groomed and trackset trails wind over the top of Wachusett's 2000-foot elevation, and offer skiers a nice view of what Indians named "the great hill." The cross-country trails are wide and well-maintained, and terrain has some spicy variety for all levels of skier. Maps, rentals, instruction, and full baselodge facilities.

ROWLEY COUNTRY CLUB SKI TOURING CENTER
Dodge Road
Rowley, Massachusetts 01969
617-948-2731

Hours: 9 a.m. to 4 p.m.
Trail System: About 15 kilometers (9 miles).
Trail Difficulty: Easiest.
Trail Grooming: Groomed and single trackset.
Rental Equipment: Yes.
Instruction: Yes.
Food Facilities: Lunches and full-service bar at the clubhouse;
    several restaurants nearby.
Lodging: Motel in Rowley with several more in Portsmouth,
    New Hampshire, about 15 miles distant.
How to Get There: I-95 north to Route 133 east; left at the
    Country Club sign.

This is a well-maintained family area very handy to Boston
and southern New Hampshire. It is laid out over the serene
terrain of a golf course. Skiers cruise over the easy-rolling
trails, across little ponds and streams, one of which is crossed
by a covered bridge. The trails begin at the club, meander over
the flats, then plunge into a nice wooded area. Back at the
clubhouse, all the amenities await, and skiers sit back before
the big fieldstone fireplace. Several family events—a scavenger
hunt race, for instance—are planned each year.

JUG END RESORT
South Egremont, Massachusetts 01258
413-528-0434

Hours: Dawn to dusk.
Trail System: 18 kilometers (about 11 miles).
Trail Difficulty: Easiest, more difficult, most difficult.
Trail Grooming: Limited.
Rental Equipment: Yes.
Instruction: No.

Food Facilities: Full-service restaurant on the premises.
Lodging: 125 rooms at the resort.
How to Get There: I-90 to Exit 2 at Lee, Massachusetts; Route
    102 west to Route 7; south through Great Barrington and
    west on Route 23 to South Egremont and Jug End.

Located in the extreme southwestern corner of the state, Jug
End has all the charm of the lower Berkshires spread out on
1,200 acres of terrain. Across the 3-mile golf course a trail loop
lets skiers warm up before plunging into a 7-mile trail network flowered out over old logging roads then plunging into
wonderful wilderness and bushwhacking. There is something
for every level and variety of skier. The Jug End Mountain
Trail feeds onto the Appalachian Trail, running north through
the Berkshires toward the Green Mountains. There are ample
accommodations at the center, and on weekend evenings at
the inn music and dancing are provided for the tireless.

OAK n' SPRUCE RESORT
South Lee, Massachusetts 01260
413-243-3500

Hours: Dawn to dusk.
Trail System: 2-mile novice loop; 50 kilometers (about 30
    miles) of trails in the adjoining state forest.
Trail Difficulty: Easiest, more difficult.
Trail Grooming: On the 2-mile novice loop.
Rental Equipment: Yes.
Instruction: Yes.
Food Facilities: Continental-style restaurant.
Lodging: 65 rooms at the resort.
How to Get There: Massachusetts Turnpike to Exit 2 in Lee;
    Route 102 south to Oak n' Spruce.

This touring center has 500 acres of open fields and a
groomed, trackset 2-mile loop. But after warming up here,
skiers plunge into the 12,000-acre Beartown State Forest and

follow the unplowed country roads, forest trails, and open-meadow touring. This is the pristine land of the whitetailed deer and wild turkey.

For beginners or serious touring skiers, Oak n' Spruce accommodates all levels. A special learn-to-ski weekend package is a good value for beginners. Accommodations—2 buildings and 65 rooms arranged in a horseshoe shape—make this a full-scale resort. Aside from group planned activities—snowshoeing, skating, and tobogganing—the area has plenty of health club-pool-sauna-Jacuzzi-cocktail lounge activity for the indoor sports.

SHERATON VILLAGE SKI TOURING CENTER
Sheraton Inn, Route 20
Sturbridge, Massachusetts 01566
617-347-9824

Hours: Monday through Friday noon to 4 p.m.; Saturday, Sunday, and school holidays 10 a.m. to 4 p.m.
Trail System: 5 kilometers (about 8 miles).
Trail Difficulty: Easiest, more difficult, most difficult.
Trail Grooming: Yes.
Rental Equipment: Yes.
Instruction: Yes.
Food Facilities: Snacks at the touring center; main-course meals at the Sheraton Sturbridge Inn.
Lodging: Sheraton Sturbridge Inn has 100 poolside rooms, 100 fireplaced rooms, and a total of 240 rooms.
How to Get There: I-90 to Exit 9; Route 20 west 1 mile to area, which is adjacent to Old Sturbridge Village.

This obviously historic region is a nice way to combine sightseeing, antiquing, and the rest with some fine ski touring on trail loops that combine much of what is best about Berkshire skiing: gentle terrain, dazzling-white open meadows, and hardwood forestland. This is the wildland of the turkey, deer, rabbit, and other small wildlife, and skiers are often startled by small apparitions in the snow.

The ability level is geared for tourers who want to ski leisurely in picturesque surroundings; the comfort level of the accommodations, however, is for anyone: swimming pool, saunas, steam rooms, and a nice cocktail lounge are waiting for the bone-weary as they come off the trail.

BUCKSTEEP MANOR TOURING CENTER

Washington Mountain Road
Washington, Massachusetts 01223
413-623-5535

Hours: 8 a.m. to 4:30 p.m.
Trail System: 25 kilometers (about 16 miles).
Trail Difficulty: Least difficult, more difficult, most difficult.
Trail Grooming: Machine trackset.
Rental Equipment: 100 sets.
Instruction: Private and group, by appointment.
Food Facilities: Manor Kitchen Restaurant on premises serves
    meals weekends and holidays. Skier Sunday Brunch special.
Lodging: Manor Inn or cabins on premises.
How to Get There: I-90 to Exit 2 at Lee; Route 20 east, then
    Route 8 north to Washington.

High atop the Berkshire Hills between October and Washington peaks, Bucksteep Manor's 1,900-foot elevation ensures one of the longest ski seasons in the region. The nicely groomed trails wind through the snow-covered fir thickets, through stream beds and bogs, and across pristine white meadows that overlook mountain valleys. Skiers can also incorporate on their tour the trail system of nearby October Mountain.

As picturesque as the land is the Manor Inn itself, a Victorian estate that serves fine homemade food in front of a big wood fire. Here are nightly entertainment and moonlight tours. Bucksteep offers citizen racing and guided tours of the Appalachian Trail.

CROSS-COUNTRY SKIING IN WAYLAND
Outdoor Education Committee
Conservation Commission
Nancy Simon Memorial Fund
Wayland, Massachusetts 01778
617-358-7701 weekdays (Jim Masik)

How to Get There: I-95 to Route 20 to Wayland.

Though many communities have open public lands for skiing, the town of Wayland has gone several steps further to provide a broad tract of well-marked wilderness skiing for those living quite near the metropolitan Boston area. Using the Nancy Simon Memorial Funds, the Outdoor Education Committee has published a series of highly detailed, waterproof trail maps and guides that give skiers not just an overall view of the terrain, but of each tree along the way as well, not to mention advice about how to dress and where to park. Though not a ski center as such, the Wayland lands have several scattered stepping-off points around town, and these are detailed in the series of the ten maps. Tours vary from the broad rolling 100-acre Snake Brook/Hamlen Woods area, to the 35-acre Pine Brook loop near the center of town. Along with the ten maps, there is an overview map and legend that provides such detail as how to identify pheasant or deer tracks along the trail. The Wayland area itself has several inns, motels, and restaurants nearby.

STUMP SPROUTS SKI TOURING
West Hill Road
West Hawley, Massachusetts 01339
413-339-4265

Hours: 9 a.m. until sunset; closed Wednesday and Thursday.
Trail System: 25 kilometers (about 16 miles).
Trail Difficulty: Easiest, most difficult.
Trail Grooming: More than 15 kilometers.
Rental Equipment: 50 sets.

Instruction: 10:30 a.m. weekend mornings, or by appointment.
Food Facilities: Snacks and hot drinks for day skiers; breakfast and dinner for lodge guests.
Lodging: Bunk-style sleeping in guest lodge.
How to Get There: I-91 to Greenfield; Route 2 west to Charlemont; south on Route 8A for 6 miles to West Hill Road; turn right for 1 mile.

Stump Sprouts is a high-elevation, rustic touring center with an eagle-eye view of the Mohawk Trail and the Berkshire wilderness. The base is a wonderful Victorian farmhouse that has a snack bar, waxing and warming room, and rental shop. A magnificent new lodge with fireplace overlooks the open countryside and provides as nice off-trail relaxation as you'll find in the Berkshire region. Skiers must make reservations for the 20-bed guest lodge, and patrons must bring their own linens and bedding.

The ski area has 15 miles of well-groomed trails that put together both open-glade touring and woodland skiing. They have such names as Easy Slider, Shakey Knees, and Lone Boulder, and range in ability level from groomed cruisers to knobby off-track stuff. There is a waxing hut and expert instruction on what to do to the bottoms of the skis and when you're on top of them. Also ask about a tour presenting a unique understanding of the ecosystem.

EAST MOUNTAIN SKI TOURING CENTER
East Mountain Country Club
East Mountain Road
Westfield, Massachusetts 01085
413-568-1539

Hours: Weekends and vacation weeks 10 a.m. to 4 p.m.
Trail System: 26 kilometers (about 15 miles).
Trail Difficulty: Easiest, more difficult, most difficult.
Trail Grooming: Groomed and trackset daily.
Rental Equipment: Yes.
Instruction: Yes.

Food Facilities: Snacks and bar at the center.

Lodging: Motels and inns in the area.

How to Get There: I-90 to West Springfield, Massachusetts; Route 20 west; just after the West Springfield-Westfield line turn right onto East Mountain Road.

Located in the vicinity of the fabled trout river by the same name, the Westfield River, this touring center begins with a marked and groomed trail system webbed over about 800 acres, then pushes out into the rural environs of these Berkshire foothills and pastures. The area of wilderness touring is loaded with wildlife from small birds to wild turkey and deer. The range of skiing is flat to very hilly and challenging in spots. East Mountain has a serviceable snack bar, with retail-rental facilities.

SHAKER FARMS
At the Shaker Farms Country Club
Shaker Road
Westfield, Massachusetts 01085
413-562-2770

Hours: 9 a.m. to 4:30 p.m.

Trail System: 25 kilometers (about 16 miles).

Trail Difficulty: Easiest, more difficult, most difficult.

Trail Grooming: Machine groomed and trackset.

Rental Equipment: 125 sets.

Instruction: Yes.

Food Facilities: Lounge/restaurant on premises.

Lodging: Motels and inns in the area.

How to Get There: Massachusetts Turnpike to Exit 3; south on Route 202 4 miles; left on Ponder Hollow Road, then take the next left, Shaker Road.

This area is laid out over a golf course and woods setting, and grooms trails meticulously for skiers. The area has nearly 400 acres of open skiing on gentle terrain, with forays off through the hardwood thickets of the Berkshire uplands. There are 5 kilometers of lighted trails as well from Monday through Sunday, and skiers can use the grounds until 10 p.m.

The area has access to many miles of skiing off the property, such as the Metacomet-Monadnock Trail along the Provin Ridge, which overlooks the Connecticut River and Westfield River valleys. This is a good area for trout fisherpersons to ski and dream of spring. The facilities include a crackling fireplace in the center of a lounge/restaurant, and moonlight excursions and citizen racing spice the pot here.

WESTON SKI TRACK
At the Leo J. Martin Golf Course
Box 426, Park Road
Weston, Massachusetts
617-894-4903

Hours: Monday through Saturday 9 a.m. to 10 p.m.; Sunday 9 a.m. to 6 p.m.
Trail System: 15 kilometers (about 9 miles).
Trail Difficulty: Easiest, more difficult.
Trail Grooming: Trackset daily.
Rental Equipment: Yes.
Instruction: PSIA-certified.
Food Facilities: Cafe and snack bar on premises.
Lodging: Many hotels and motels in the area.
How to Get There: I-90 to Exit 15, onto I-95; north to Route 30, then west to a left turn onto Park Road and to Weston Ski Track.

As cross-country skiing caught on among greater Bostonians during the last two decades, a need arose for local areas near the city. Mike Farny and The Lincoln Guide Service, given a shove by M.R. Montgomery of *The Boston Globe*, opened the Weston Track on a popular MDC golf course. Since those origins in the early 1970s, the area has grown as a place to work out, to get excellent lessons, and to practice for the trips upcountry.

And lest ye think Weston sounds rather small and insignificant, you'll encounter some of the serious folks in the sport here, wearing their one-piece body suits and zinging around the loops at 15 miles an hour. Here high school and college teams work out over the carefully groomed tracks. The addition of snowmaking makes it possible to ski here even when there's no snow in the flatlands. After a workout, skiers relax in the Langlaufer Cafe, whose name translates: "Cross-country skiers live longer." There are showers, lockers, waxing areas, and full retail shop. It goes without saying, there are plenty of citizen's races at the track, as well as clinics on everything from waxing to skating technique.

NOTCHVIEW RESERVATION
Route 9
Windsor, Massachusetts 01262
413-684-0148

Hours: Dawn to dusk from December 1 through March 1.
Trail System: 25 kilometers (about 16 miles).
Trail Difficulty: Easiest, more difficult, most difficult.
Trail Grooming: On the main trail only.
Rental Equipment: No.
Instruction: None.
Food Facilities: Picnic room, and several restaurants within 5 miles.
Lodging: Several motels and inns within 5 miles in Windsor and Stockbridge.
How to Get There: Massachusetts Turnpike to Lee; Route 7 north to Pittsfield, Massachusetts; then Route 9 east for about 14 miles to Notchview.

Many knowledgeable cross-country aficionados consider Notchview one of the best wilderness ski areas in the Berkshires, with its 25-kilometer spider web of trails for every level of skiing challenge. Main loops plunge along through this spruce forest so appreciated by small game, deer, and a growing flock of wild turkeys. Ancient stone walls and cellar holes poignantly bespeak a rugged farming history. Part of the Hoosac Range, Notchview Reservation has a system of trails running over old fire and logging roads, with clear difficulty-leveling signs at each intersection.

The main loop, Circuit Trail, leads to a pasture with a sudden vista of the notch, cut by Shaw Brook, a tributary of the Westfield River. It is this view that gives the area its name. A most challenging trail is a steep climb up Judges Hill, rising to 2,300 feet, the highest point in Windsor. The snow comes early here and hangs in late because of the spruce shade. Budds Visitors Center is on the premises with rest rooms, a picnic room with a big fireplace, and a waxing room. Notchview is one of 69 properties owned by the Trustees of Reservations, a private, non-profit organization founded in 1891 to preserve beautiful and historic places in Massachusetts.

HICKORY HILL TOURING CENTER
Box 39
Buffington Hill Road
Worthington, Massachusetts 01098
413-238-5813

Hours: 9 a.m. to dusk.
Trail System: 40 kilometers (about 25 miles).
Trail Difficulty: Easiest, more difficult, and most difficult.
Trail Grooming: Machine double trackset.
Rental Equipment: Yes.
Instruction: Yes.
Food Facilities: Food service in the barn on weekends.
Lodging: Inns and motels in the area within 20 miles.
How to Get There: I-91 to Northampton; Route 9 northwest to
    Route 143; west on Route 112 and Worthington, then right
    onto Buffington Hill Road.

With an expanded trail system, good elevation (1,800 feet) to
ensure long seasons, and improvements each year, Hickory
Hill is developing as a popular ski center in the Berkshires.

The 40 kilometers of groomed, trackset, and well-marked
trails are spread out over 700 acres of old New England farm
country and adjoining hardwood forests. The rolling meadowland is interlaced with old colonial stone walls, and in spots
skiers are treated to lovely overlooks of 40 miles and more out
toward New York state. Hickory Hill offers a special package
for beginners. Maps and trail guides are available. The barn
serves beverages, baked goods, and a soup du jour in front of a
constantly roaring fireplace. There is a fulsome schedule of
moonlight and maple sugar tours, as well as an old-fashioned
pig roast in mid-season.

VERMONT

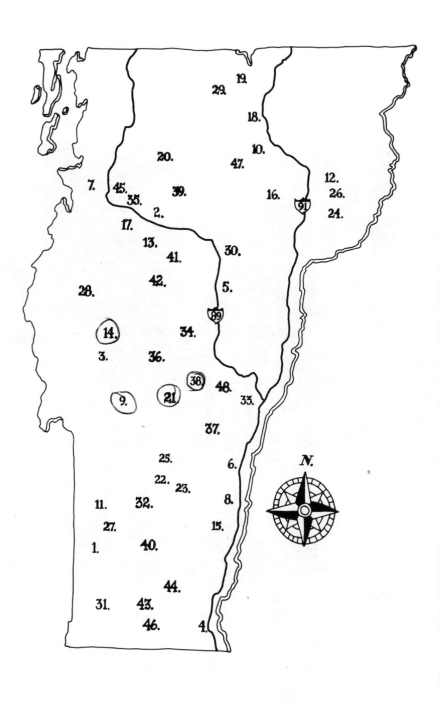

Vermont

Numbers on map refer to towns numbered below

THE WEST MOUNTAIN INN
Route 313, River Road
Arlington, Vermont 05250
802-375-6516

Hours: Daylight.
Trail System: 9 kilometers (about 5 miles).
Trail Difficulty: Easiest, more difficult, most difficult.
Trail Grooming: None; wilderness trails.
Rental Equipment: None.
Instruction: None.
Food Facilities: Breakfast, 8 a.m. to 10 a.m.; dinner 7 p.m. by
    reservation only.
Lodging: Rooms and cottages at the inn.
How to Get There: Route I-91 to Brattleboro, Vermont; Route 9
    west to Bennington; Route 7 north to Arlington, then
    Route 313 west to West Mountain Road, and up the hill.

This wilderness area is the best sort of Vermont inn—hidden
in the splendidly intimate surroundings of the Batten Kill
River woodlands. From the door of the inn skiers overlook the
famous Batten Kill with its trout-fishing lore, then begin to
work off breakfast first on the easy flats, then on the seemingly
endless ruggedness of the old logging trails. Some of these
trails can get woolly and steep, but they are quite wide. Back
nearer the inn is a wonderful all-purpose hill for Telemark
practice or moonlight tobogganing.

At night at the inn you'll find in front of the huge fire just
as fine cuisine as there is in Vermont, starting with hot drinks
and cocktails, an artistic meal, and after-dinner activity
around the piano. There are 13 rooms, cottages, and a 2-bed-
room housekeeping apartment as well.

BOLTON VALLEY CROSS COUNTRY CENTER
Bolton Valley Ski Resort
Bolton, Vermont 05477
802-434-2131

Hours: 9 a.m. to 4 p.m.
Trail System: More than 100 kilometers (60 miles).
Trail Difficulty: Easiest, more difficult, most difficult.
Trail Grooming: 10 kilometers rolled and trackset; 20 kilometers rolled; remainder, wilderness skiing.
Rental Equipment: Yes.
Instruction: Beginning group to private Telemark.
Food Facilities: 8 separate dining experiences.
Lodging: Bolton Valley Lodge has an 85-bed capacity; other motels and inns in the area.
How to Get There: I-95 to I-89 to Exit 10; Route 2 and Bolton access road to the ski area.

Bolton Valley's gentle Alpine slopes work well to the ski tourer's advantage. The area has a very well-developed Nordic trail system set into the 2,100-foot elevation, and that means snow—lots of it—well into April most years. But take advantage of Bolton's downhill capability, and you will become an expert Telemarker as well. Skiers begin with the Sitzmark Trail, graduate to the intermediate Telemark trail, they try Cliffhanger, where the trail system works into the Trapp Family Lodge and Mt. Mansfield—a trek for experts. Skiers taking this route or any other may take the group lessons available at Bolton Valley beginning at 10 a.m. Aside from a full-complement retail and rental shop, Bolton Valley has all the amenities of a major downhill ski area, and cross-country tourers are welcome as well.

CHURCHILL HOUSE INN AND SKI TOURING CENTER
Route 73
Brandon, Vermont 05733
802-247-3300

Hours: 10 a.m. to 4 p.m.
Trail System: 40 kilometers (about 25 miles).
Trail Difficulty: Easiest, more difficult, most difficult.
Trail Grooming: 20 kilometers groomed and trackset daily.
Rental Equipment: Yes.
Instruction: Yes.
Food Facilities: Dining for guests; other restaurants within 5 miles.
Lodging: 9 rooms at the inn with many hotels and motels in the area.
How to Get There: I-91 to I-89 west; Route 4 west to Rutland, Vermont; Route 7 north to Brandon; then Route 73 east to Churchill House.

Churchill House is part of a four-lodge, five-day inn-to-inn trip from north to south that lets skiers get some real miles under the boards traveling from Bristol to Chittenden. Churchill is a stout, three-story farmhouse of the Civil War period, and preserves the century-old feel inside and out. The trail system begins with groomed and trackset loops of flattish terrain near the inn, then flowers out into some rugged wilderness challenge. Along several of the trail systems, skiers get sudden vistas of the Adirondacks. The system winds into the Green Mountain National Forest and its nearly limitless skiing. Back at the inn, with its full fare of cocktails and gourmet dining, skiers find rentals and retail available, guided tours, and organized events. In the waxing hut through the day, hot soup and bread is always available to see one through to the inn's sumptuous meals.

BRATTLEBORO OUTING CLUB SKI HUT
Box 335, Upper Dummerston Road
Brattleboro, Vermont 05301
802-254-4081 or 603-399-4886

Hours: 9 a.m. to 4 p.m.
Trail System: 15 kilometers (about 9 miles).
Trail Difficulty: Easiest, more difficult.
Trail Grooming: All trails.
Rental Equipment: Yes.
Instruction: By appointment.
Food Facilities: 2 miles distant in Brattleboro.
Lodging: In Brattleboro.
How to Get There: I-93 to Brattleboro to second exit; Route 30
    to Upper Dummerston Road to the Outing Club.

This wide-open ski area is spread out across an 18-hole golf
course and the nearby woodlands. The trails are groomed, and
used often by the more athletic of the cross-country fraternity.
Some trails cross bridges and skirt ponds, others are flat runners along the fairways. The system is anchored by a center
with ski shop, warming hut, rentals, retail goods, and snacks.
Skiers here can also sign up for moonlight excursions.

GREEN TRAILS INN & SKI TOURING CENTER
Pond Village
Brookfield, Vermont 05036
802-276-3412

Hours: 9 a.m. to 5 p.m.
Trail System: 40 kilometers (about 25 miles).
Trail Difficulty: Easiest, more difficult, most difficult.
Trail Grooming: Machine groomed and trackset.
Rental Equipment: Yes.
Instruction: PSIA-certified instructors by appointment at the
    inn.
Food Facilities: Breakfast and dinner at the center's restau-
    rant; lunches available to skiers.

Lodging: 15 rooms at the inn.

How to Get There: I-91 to I-89, northeast to Vermont Exit 4; Route 66 east to Randolph Center, then north for 7½ miles to Brookfield. Signs to the center.

Green Trails Inn & Ski Touring Center is an area that keeps evolving around what was once nineteenth-century farmland in the historic village of Brookfield, Vermont. Encompassing a restored farmhouse and two other residences, the center offers 15 nice rooms with plenty of Victorian and early American flavor. The ski trail system keeps expanding over the rolling pastureland, frozen lakes, and hills of the region; one trail takes skiers across the famed floating bridge over a narrow pond. Skating, snowshoeing, and sleigh rides complete this winter postcard scene. The trail system itself incorporates other nearby trail systems for plenty of skiing—including the Allis State Park on 400 acres of groomed and wilderness trail. The center has complete rental and retail offerings, and the food is homemade and delicious.

ASCUTNEY MOUNTAIN RESORT TOURING CENTER
Route 44
Brownsville, Vermont 05037
802-484-7711 or 800-243-0011

Hours: Saturday, Sunday, all holidays, vacation weeks 8:30 a.m. to 4 p.m.

Trail System: 32 kilometers (about 20 miles).

Trail Difficulty: Easiest, more difficult, most difficult.

Trail Grooming: Daily.

Rental Equipment: Yes.

Instruction: Yes.

Food Facilities: Cafeteria at the Ascutney Alpine area nearby.

Lodging: Inns and motels in the area.

How to Get There: I-91 to Route 44 in Vermont; west to the touring center.

This broad plateau looks down on the white-steepled village of Brownsville, and beyond to the pretty white swaths of the

Ascutney Alpine area, a tall tower of a peak. For tourers, the surroundings are lumpy and very pretty—the essence of Vermont's Green Mountain countryside. The 32 kilometers of trail undulate through this land over pasture, along stream bed, and through deep fir thickets. Nearly all of it is gentle until you take the guided backcountry tours—including overnight trips by arrangement—at which point the skiing becomes a bit of challenge. At the warming hut and rental shop, skiers can arrange for lessons.

THE CATAMOUNT TRAIL ASSOCIATION
Box 897
Burlington, Vermont 05402

The core of the Catamount Trail Association (CTA) is a group of fanatic skiers who trekked the length of Vermont in March 1984, and who now dedicate themselves to the proposition that all skiers could and should ski on North America's longest trail—from Massachusetts to Quebec.

Steve Bushey, Paul Jarris, and Ben Rose hatched the idea that, by linking the trails of several touring areas together with old roads along the ridge line of the Green Mountains, the entire length of the state can be easily traversed. The route selected is a skiing nirvana: a trail that runs through deep woods and open fields; over long descents down forgotten roads, over clearings with sudden views of mountain and valley, and down into amiable New England villages as you trek along north. The largest part of this "winter-long" trail, as its creators call it, is already accessible to skiers in the form of unplowed roads connected to groomed ski center trails and other public ways. However, there are several sections that still must be cleared, and Catamount Trail Association members—present and future—are about the task. Anyone who joins CTA (write the address) will be kept informed of developments by newsletter.

With an average elevation of between 1,500 and 2,000 feet, the trail system will have reliable snow cover, and will constitute a skiing resource for every level of Nordic aficionado. The trail begins at the White House in Wilmington, Vermont, and roughly parallels Route 100 up to Hermitage, Stratton, Nordic Inn, then the Village Inn outside of Londonderry. The trek then pushes north over the Green Mountains toward Rutland, where it picks up Mountain Meadows near Killington; then Mountain Top, Blueberry Hill, Sugarbush, Tucker Hill, Camel's Hump, and the Trapp Family Lodge at Stowe along with Mansfield. From Mansfield, the tour pushes up on the 10th Army Mountain road to Top Notch, Edson Hill, Craftsbury, Hazen's Notch, and onto its terminus at Jay Peak.

Individual memberships in CTA are $10 annually, and $20 for business or organization memberships, payable to the address above.

SKI TOURS OF VERMONT
RFD 1
Chester, Vermont 05143
802-824-6012

How to Get There: Massachusetts Turnpike to I-91 exit; follow to Route 11 in Vermont.

Rather than a particular destination, Ski Tours of Vermont is a guide and instruction service in the National Forest of Weston and Londonderry, Vermont. Tours access the Great Vermont Ski Trail, and offer personalized outfitting and instruction. Treks vary from three days to eight days, and put together inn-to-inn touring—the ultimate in the trekking end of the sport—at its very best. Aside from the variety of terrain as you ski through the Green Mountains, you will stay at country inns—from old New England farmhouses to former country gentlemen's estates—and sample all sorts of cuisines, from French to Swiss, to genuine New England. Meanwhile your luggage is sent along to your next stop. Like most ski guide services, Ski Tours will match a trip to the skier's ability, experience, and taste. But make plans early.

76

TATER HILL CROSS-COUNTRY SKI CENTER
Chester, Vermont 05143
802-875-2517

Hours: 9:00 a.m. to 4:30 p.m.
Trail System: 40 kilometers (about 25 miles).
Trail Difficulty: Easiest, more difficult, most difficult.
Trail Grooming: Over about 20 kilometers.
Rental Equipment: Yes.
Instruction: Yes.
Food Facilities: On the premises.
Lodging: Within three miles.
How to Get There: Follow I-91 to Exit 6; Route 103 north to
    Chester; then Route 11 west to the center, between Ches-
    ter and Londonderry.

Tater Hill Center is a good sized trail system surrounding a 200-year-old farmhouse in central Vermont. It offers good skiing on groomed trails, as well as some real wilderness experience breaking trail as you ski out to the tough Williams River loop. To get your bearings first, the Whitetail and Sweet Potater trails are flat running loops, both of which pass warming shelters along the way. Most trails pass through hardwood forest with some nice views of the rolling Green Mountain foothills. Back at the inn food and drink are available in the post-Revolutionary flavor of so many Vermont inns. Through the season there are several races organized along with the annual Scandinavian Night, a moonlight cruise followed by an embarrassment of caloric riches at the smorgasbord table.

Very difficult; don't recommend unless ex. cellent skier

MOUNTAIN TOP SKI TOURING CENTER
Chittenden, Vermont 05737
802-445-2100 (reservations) and 802-483-6089 (snow phone)

Hours: 9 a.m. to 5 p.m.
Trail System: 110 kilometers (about 70 miles).
Trail Difficulty: Easiest, more difficult, most difficult.
Trail Grooming: 30 to 40 kilometers are groomed and double
    trackset daily.

Rental Equipment: 125 sets.

Instruction: PSIA-certified.

Food Facilities: Snack bar at the touring center; full-service restaurant at the Mountain Top Inn.

Lodging: Mountain Top Inn, a full-service hotel with 50 rooms.

How to Get There: I-93 to I-89; take Exit 1 and Route 4 west to Rutland. Follow signs for Mountain Top Ski Touring just past the entrance to Pico Peak.

Just when you think you've seen all of Vermont's country inn and ski touring, there is another inn, another area more beautiful than the last. That's the first impression one takes from Mountain Top with its enormous trail system that winds out through dazzling white meadows and quiet hardwood forestland. The elevation—2,000 feet—gives Mountain Top excellent capacity to hold snow as well as some stunning panoramic views of the peaks and lakes of the Green Mountain National Forest. In addition, Mountain Top makes its own snow on a 5-kilometer track loop that is a fine warm-up and exercise area for all ability levels. Beyond that, there is skiing over the gently rolling Alpine meadows and spruce forest, and then some toe-curling challenge for experts over tough, twisting, choppy trails with steep verticals. The ski season holds well into the spring here.

At day's end, the Ski Shop, a converted horse barn warmed by a big woodstove, has a full compement of retail and rental gear, hot soups, drinks, and snacks. There is also a sundeck for the mild days. Skiers can sign up here for lessons, waxing and racing clinics, seminars and films. Remember that the area is near two big downhill centers (Pico and Killington), so visitors should seek advance reservations.

CRAFTSBURY NORDIC SKI CENTER
Box 81
Craftsbury Common, Vermont 05827
802-586-2514

Hours: 7 a.m. to 5 p.m. (night skiing under the lights).
Trail System: 30 kilometers (about 19 miles).
Trail Difficulty: Easiest, more difficult.
Trail Grooming: Daily.
Rental Equipment: Yes.
Instruction: Private and group lessons.
Food Facilities: Buffet-style dining—three meals.
Lodging: Ski dorm, apartments, and 50 other units at the center.
How to Get There: I-89 to Montpelier, Vermont; Route 14 to Craftsbury.

Located in one of the wildest stretches of New England—the Northeast Kingdom—Craftsbury's 30 kilometers of trails are groomed to a fault, and maintained for race training as well as casual recreational skiing. The trail system winds into others maintained in the Northeast Kingdom, so skiers can access about 85 kilometers. Used more by racers than tourers is one 12-mile loop that winds up out of Craftsbury Valley to a wood-stove-heated warming hut. At the center is a ski dorm with 34 bedrooms, along with 4 apartments and a cottage for rent. The center, often buzzing with race activity, has all the amenities for serious skiing. A bit less spartan housing is found at the Inn on the Common, where guests are granted free access to the trails at the Center. Children are welcome at all facilities at Craftsbury.

BARROWS HOUSE
Dorset, Vermont 05251
802-867-4455

Hours: 9 a.m. to 6 p.m.
Trail System: 8 kilometers (about 5 miles).
Trail Difficulty: Easiest, more difficult.

Trail Grooming: No.
Rental Equipment: Yes.
Instruction: Yes.
Food Facilities: Dining room at the inn.
Lodging: Rooms at the inn.
How to Get There: I-91 to Brattleboro, Vermont; Route 9 west to Bennington; Route 7 north to Route 30, then northwest to Dorset and Barrows House.

Barrows House is one of those ski touring areas one might, with humility, term "mellow." Centered around a Revolutionary-period inn with all the wonderful amenities of big roaring fireplaces and candlelit dining room, the touring center combines low-stress trekking with some nicely groomed flat tracks that exercise freaks will enjoy right along with the duffers. Trails spread out from the inn, run through moderately sloped wooded terrain that can get the heart pumping; skiers then cross frozen streams and open meadowland. For the adventurous, just a few minutes distant lies the 2,700-acre Merek Forest, which will take you to lovely overlooks of the Taconic Hills and the Adirondacks. Amenities here at Barrows House are laudable, beginning with a big breakfast and a packed lunch for the trail. Awaiting your return is a sauna, a crackling-fireside drink, and gourmet dinner. This area provides the total touring experience for perhaps 90 percent of the market.

BURKE MOUNTAIN SKI TOURING CENTER
Box 101
East Burke, Vermont 05832
802-626-8338

Hours: 9 a.m. to sunset.
Trail System: 50 kilometers (about 31 miles).
Trail Difficulty: Easiest, more difficult, most difficult.
Trail Grooming: Yes.
Rental Equipment: Yes.
Instruction: PSIA-certified.
Food Facilities: At touring center.
Lodging: At nearby inns and condominiums.
How to Get There: I-91 north to Exit 23; Route 5 to Route 114 to
    East Burke; signs to Burke Mountain.

This historic center for Alpine athletes (Burke Ski Academy) also maintains a well-developed touring center over the rolling meadows and deep Vermont woodlands near the Northeast Wilderness Kingdom. Most of the trail system is intermediate, though those same trails have been used for National Cross-Country Championships. From some high-country views, skiers look out for miles to the west, and the striking scenery of Willoughby Gap, gateway to the Northeast Kingdom. Skiers may use any trail system here, and wind back to the center. The Touring Center itself is a friendly, bustling stop in an old restored farmhouse with a radiant woodstove at its center. Here skiers may sip hot cider and homemade soups, rent equipment, buy retail goods, and seek instruction. Children are welcome both at the touring center and at the Cutter Inn, in the midst of the trail network.

MAD RIVER BARN CROSS-COUNTRY TRAILS
Route 17
Fayston, Vermont 05673
802-496-6550 or 802-496-3551

Hours: 8 a.m. to 5 p.m.
Trail System: About 15 kilometers (about 10 miles).
Trail Difficulty: Easiest.
Trail Grooming: Groomed and double trackset.
Rental Equipment: Yes.
Instruction: Cross-country and Telemark with PSIA-certified
    instructors.
Food Facilities: 3 meals daily.
Lodging: 15 rooms.
How to Get There: I-89 to Route 100 at Middlesex, Vermont,
    through Waitsfield to Route 17 west for 4 miles.

From the Mad River Barn, near the famous Alpine ski area of
the same name, skiers kick out over the gentle terrain into the
quiet Vermont woods, among birch, maple, and spruce with
the snowy wisps of birches among them. Frozen streams,
stone walls through ancient orchards—this is classic New England landscape, lovely and unspoiled. It is an excellent area
for beginning skiers, and the experienced can get the old heart
pumping with some fast runs down the Beaver Loop, and back
out the Farm Loop. A logging road takes skiers to Mad River
Glen Alpine are for some Telemark practice. Back at the barn,
skiers find full rental and retail gear, and a good big area for
warming and waxing. Some trails are lighted for night skiing.

BLUEBERRY HILL *Recommended by*
Goshen, Vermont 05733 *Trail Head Ski*
802-247-6735 or 800-247-6535 *Resort people*

Hours: 8 a.m. to dark.
Trail System: 50 to 75 kilometers, depending on snow cover
    and forestry activity in the National Forest.
Trail Difficulty: Easiest, more difficult, most difficult.

Trail Grooming: All trails groomed and double trackset.
Rental Equipment: Yes.
Instruction: Private and group rates.
Food Facilities: Soup included in the trail fee, along with "munchies," but you'd better bring your own packed lunches and other meals.
Lodging: Blueberry Hill is connected with a small inn.
How to Get There: I-91 to I-89 west to Route 4, west to Rutland, Vermont; north on route 7 to Brandon, east on Route 73 to Goshen, then left at the town hall to Blueberry Hill.

Blueberry Hill, nestled in the Green Mountain National Forest with an honest 50- to 70-kilometer trail system, is a major ski area for the serious tourer as well as the hiker searching for gorgeous mountain overlooks that plunge into deep forestland with snow-laden fir boughs and frozen brooks. Silver Lake trail is a good way to get your legs, then stretch out along Long Trail for more challenging skiing. There is an excellent retail and rental shop at Blueberry, along with waxing rooms where some helpful lessons are taught. The inn is small—just 8 rooms—but the space is worth fighting for.

Ask for Steve Buskey or owner Tony Clark for special advice about skiing conditions.

GRAFTON CROSS-COUNTRY SKI SHOP AND TRAIL SYSTEM

Townshend Road
Grafton, Vermont 05146
802-843-2234

Hours: 9:30 to 4:30.
Trail System: 40 kilometers (about 25 miles).
Trail Difficulty: Easiest, more difficult, most difficult.
Trail Grooming: Daily.
Rental Equipment: Yes.
Instruction: Private and group lessons available.
Food Facilities: The Old Tavern is just one-half mile distant.
Lodging: A variety of inns and motels in the area.

How to Get There: I-91 to Brattleboro, Vermont; Route 30 northwest to Route 35; north into Grafton.

Jud and Gretchen Hartmann are proprietors of this wonderful touring area with its genuine old-world, kerosene-lamp feel. The wood fire-warmed log cabin at the foot of Bear Hill houses the ski shop where you'll kick off onto the 40-kilometer trail system with its one Green Mountain oddity: an abundance of blessed flat land. There is instruction for beginner and expert alike. The trail system, in part, loops along the Saxtons River, then mounts into Beaver Pond Trail Loop, a good runner for exercise-seekers, and also a fine hiking trail as well. This is small, rustic, extremely picturesque skiing and lodging at its New England best.

HIGHLAND LODGE
Caspian Lake
Greensboro, Vermont 05841
802-533-2647

Hours: 9 a.m. to 5 p.m.
Trail System: About 48 kilometers (30 miles).
Trail Difficulty: Easiest, more difficult.
Trail Grooming: All 30 miles is roller-packed, five feet in width; 10 miles is single trackset.
Rental Equipment: Yes.
Instruction: PSIA certified.
Food Facilities: Full meals plus trail snacks in the ski shop.
Lodging: 11 rooms at the lodge and two cottages.
How to Get There: I-91 to St. Johnsbury; at Exit 15, Route 2 west 10 miles to West Danville; northwest on Route 15 to Route 16; north on Route 16 to East Hardwick, then west to Greensboro.

There are three loops to Highland Lodge's trail system, two of 5 miles and another of 15 miles. All of these course through the gently rolling pasturelands and evergreen woods that lead down and sweep the shore of Caspian Lake. The system covers

about 25 square miles. Both loops offer some wonderful overlooks of this lake region, and end with a downhill stretch
toward a drink at the fireplace. The trails are conscientiously
roller-packed so skiers don't have to bushwhack their way
through deep powder or crust.

The lodge is a spectacular stately Vermont inn with a
broad homey dining room, library and lounge areas, and good-
size double bedrooms. There is room for 35 guests. The inn
hosts loyal families that have been returning for several years.
There is also a thorough ski and rental shop at the center
where skiers may sign up for instruction and guided tours of
the region.

CAMEL'S HUMP NORDIC SKI CENTER
Box 99, RFD 1
Huntington, Vermont 05462
802-434-2704

Hours: Saturday, Sunday, and holiday weeks, 9 a.m. to 5 p.m.
Trail System: 50 kilometers (31 miles).
Trail Difficulty: Easiest, more difficult, most difficult.
Trail Grooming: Daily.
Rental Equipment: Yes.
Instruction: Yes.
Food Facilities: Meals served at the center.
Lodging: In Huntington Center, within 2 miles, and in Jones-
    ville.
How to Get There: I-91 to I-89 northwest to Exit 11; Route 117
    south to Huntington; take East Street to the touring cen-
    ter.

Of all Vermont's high Alpine ski touring, this Nordic Ski Center just may provide the most dramatic and unusual experience. Though the center itself is a modest, family-run
operation, it is located at road's end high in the eastern foothills of the 4,000-foot Camel's Hump, and accesses many miles
of wilderness as well as providing its own well-groomed trail
system of about 30 miles. Here is skiing for everyone: the high-

energy seeker of wilderness adventure can find guided overnight trips to a snow cave. One trail, the Honey Hollow Ski
Trail, climbs to 1,900 feet, then drops 1,500 feet over the west
slope on a non-stop downhill run of 9 kilometers to the bank of
the Winooski River in Bolton. Skiers needn't climb back up
this 5-mile rush through the state forest; the center provides
shuttle service back home again. The center intends to complete soon a network of trail huts for overnight skiers who can
travel south to Breadloaf and Blueberry Hill.

For gentler spirits not looking for quite this level of stimu-
lation, the center has plenty of cruising on flatter trails
through woods and open mountain uplands. All rentals and
retail needs, along with meals, are taken care of in the rustic
center, which now also provides lodging.

HEERMANSMITH FARM
RFD 1
Irasburg (Coventry Village), Vermont 05845
802-754-8866

Hours: 9 a.m. to 4 p.m.
Trail System: 15 kilometers (about 9½ miles) with three con-
    nected trails.
Trail Difficulty: Easiest, more difficult, most difficult.
Trail Grooming: Groomed and trackset daily.
Rental Equipment: Yes.
Instruction: Weekends; PSIA-certified instructors.
Food Facilities: Dinners open to public nightly except Tuesday;
    lunch and breakfast served to guests only.
Lodging: Three rooms available at the farm.
How to Get There: I-91 to Orleans exit, then north along Route
    5 for 5 miles to Coventry Village; the inn is one-quarter
    mile beyond.

Heermansmith Farm is 25 miles from the Jay Peak ski area in
the remote wilds of northern Vermont. Like the other medium-sized Nordic areas in this region, the farm offers a real
variety of groomed tracks and bushwhacking terrain. Former

U.S. Ski Team member Stan Dunklee designed the trackset course with its three interconnected trail loops. Starting with the meadow trail cut along flats for a 2-kilometer run, skiers can take off along the Black River trail that winds along the lovely trout stream, in and out of sun-dappled fir forest. Then for most serious runners there is the 6-kilometer trail that takes you 2 kilometers uphill, then 4 kilometers that wind down a gentle slope through maple orchards. Heermansmith offers 5- and 10-kilometer races during Winterfest in the town of Newport, usually in February. On Sunday evenings, 2 kilometers of trail near the Farm are lighted with luminaries.

JAY PEAK SKI AREA
Route 242
Jay, Vermont 05859
802-988-2611 (Customer Service)

Hours: 8:30 a.m. to dusk.
Trail System: About 22 kilometers (13 miles).
Trail Difficulty: Easiest, more difficult, most difficult.
Trail Grooming: Yes, limited.
Rental Equipment: Yes.
Instruction: PSIA-certified.
Food Facilities: Cafeteria and 2 restaurants.
Lodging: Hotel Jay. Call Jay Peak Lodging Association at 800-548-5300 or 802-988-4363.
How to Get There: I-91 to Exit 26 in Orleans, Vermont; northwest via Routes 5 to 14 to 100, to 101, and to 242 and the entrance.

With its multinational flag row, its mix of languages and cultures, and its large Alpine facility, Jay Peak in the northernmost tip of the state in the Wilderness Kingdom, is a most exciting place to spend a ski weekend or vacation. The extensive cross-country trail system incorporates the lower half of Jay Mountain itself, which brings into play some long, gradually pitched Alpine runouts from mid-mountain down to the base. Obviously, Jay is a fine place to work on Telemark skiing, for then skiers can make use of the entire area—including two T-bars (included in trail fee) when none of your cross-country purist pals are watching. The baselodge and restaurant at the Hotel Jay is ample and well stocked. As a diversion from skiing, take the aerial tram to the top for one of the most overwhelming mountain vistas anywhere, as you view the sun dropping toward the Laurentians and Montreal. Don't worry— if you're not up to skiing down the mountain on skinny skiis, you may take the tram back down.

RED FOX SKI TOURING CENTER
Old Route 108, Box 26
Jeffersonville, Vermont 05464
802-644-8888

Hours: from 8 a.m. to 4 p.m.
Trail System: 3 kilometers from Red Fox to Smugglers Notch Ski Touring Area; 2 kilometers along the Brewster River; 17 kilometers from Smugglers Notch to Pleasant Valley. A brief bus ride accesses all the trails of Stowe.
Trail Difficulty: Easiest, more difficult.
Trail Grooming: None.
Rental Equipment: 25 sets; snowshoes.
Instruction: Yes.
Food Facilities: Breakfast and dinner at the Red Fox Lodge and Dormitory.
Lodging: At the lodge; the ski dorm sleeps 146, six to eight in a room.
How to Get There: I-89 from Burlington, Vermont, to Exit 15 east; Route 108 south for 4 miles to Red Fox on the left.

Along the Old Mountain road on the way to Smugglers Notch in the northern expanse of the state, a converted church has long served as one of the original ski dormitories in the awesome landscape of Smugglers Notch. This is historic ski country where the 10th Mountain Army Division trained, and where early ski pioneers still live today.

The Red Fox Dormitory itself accesses several trail systems, specializes in group accommodations for up to 140 skiers in nice clean rooms of six to twelve beds each. The Red Fox places heavy emphasis on teaching the sport both over trails and in the surrounding wilderness settings. This is an excellent region for backcountry bushwhacking, and even some extensive—carefully-planned—wilderness treks. All of Smugglers' and Stowe's trail system is at your disposal, and if you happen to commit Alpine skiing, you're in one of the capitals of the Northeast.

CORTINA INN
Killington, Vermont 05751
802-773-3331

Hours: 9 a.m. to dusk.
Trail System: 45 kilometers (about 28 miles).
Trail Difficulty: Easiest, more difficult, most difficult.
Trail Grooming: No.
Rental Equipment: No.
Instruction: Yes, through a health club at the inn.
Food Facilities: Restaurant at the inn; lunches and trail snacks available.
Lodging: Rooms at the inn.
How to Get There: I-91 to I-89 west to Route 4 west to Killington.

Despite the abundance of Vermont's red-barn-in-the-distance rustic inns, there is an alternative for those skiers seeking the uncompromisingly modern après-ski life in all its contemporary luxury. The inn is elegant, with a wonderful wine cellar, award-winning cuisine all within a sort of modern art gallery for Vermont artists. Begin the evening in front of one of three huge fires at the inn. Cocktails at Theodore's Lounge is the usual way to begin the evening war stories. After the meal, a massage, sauna, and plunge in the warmed indoor pool smoothes out those aching muscles just a bit. Cross-country spartans may feel a bit out of place is such opulence, but then, after a breakfast of Waffles Cortina or Eggs Hussard, it's time to get running out on the very extensive trail system. This well-marked and groomed spider-web network of nearly 30 miles links together with trail systems from several other inns in the area, as well as the state forest. This latter is difficult skiing that will require some late-day pampering. Most of Cortina's own trails are woodland winders that follow ancient logging roads across streams, and into sudden views of towering Pico Peak. Snowshoes are also available to rent.

Don't recommend !

MOUNTAIN MEADOWS SKI TOURING CENTER
Killington, Vermont 05751   *Very busy; very*
802-775-7077   *difficult*

Hours: 9 a.m. to 5 p.m.
Trail System: 24 kilometers (15 miles).
Trail Difficulty: Easiest, more difficult, most difficult.
Trail Grooming: Regularly.
Rental Equipment: Yes.
Instruction: PSIA-certified.
Food Facilities: Lunches and snacks at the center.
Lodging: Dormitory and private rooms at the center.
How to Get There: I-93 to I-89 to Exit 2, then west on Route 4 to
    Killington; right on Thundering Brook Road to Mountain
    Meadows.

Nestled in a high mountain valley 5 miles away from the famous Killington downhill area, the Mountain Meadows Lodge is a large century-old converted farmhouse and barn that now can accommodate 70 tourers. The trail network, combining the depths of the Green Mountain National Forest with open mountain highlands and the flats of Kent's Pond, has offerings for every ability level. The adventurous can pick up the route along the 40-mile Vermont Ski Touring Trail, and follow it into Chittenden to the Mountain Top Ski Touring Center. The shop

at Mountain Meadows is fully equipped with rentals and retail gear, wax room and good advice. Skiers can sign up here for day or moonlight tours. Beginners should ask about the Five-Day-Learn-to-Ski-Week. Two kilometers near the lodge are lighted for some night running.

NORDIC INN SKI TOURING CENTER
Route 11
Landgrove, Vermont 05148
802-824-6444

Hours: 9 a.m. to 4 p.m.
Trail System: About 20 kilometers (12 plus miles).
Trail Difficulty: Easiest, more difficult, most difficult.
Trail Grooming: Daily.
Rental Equipment: 50 sets.
Instruction: Yes.
Food Facilities: Restaurant and pub at the inn.

Lodging: 5 rooms at the inn; other motels nearby.
How to Get There: I-91 to Exit 6; Route 103 northwest; then
    Route 11 west to Landgrove and the inn.

With its Scandinavian flair, gourmet dining, and pub life, Nordic Inn is becoming as well known for its après-ski life as for its excellent trail system. The latter, a thoroughly groomed and trackset web of trails at over 1200 feet, leads skiers into the Green Mountain National Forest, where plenty of wilderness skiing is at hand. The inn offers a full service of guided tours, instruction, and various events through the season. After a day on these broad, hardwood-lined trails, skiers stretch in front of the huge fieldstone fireplace that crackles and roars through the long winter evening. This is a fine destination area for those who like some pampering when they're off the trails. Nordic Inn is just three miles from Londonderry, and five miles from the Bromley downhill ski area.

VIKING SKI TOURING CENTER
Little Pond Road
Londonderry, Vermont 05148
802-824-3933

Hours: 8:30 a.m. to 5 p.m.
Trail System: 45 kilometers (about 28 miles).
Trail Difficulty: Easiest, more difficult, most difficult.
Trail Grooming: Yes.
Rental Equipment: 130 sets.
Instruction: PSIA-certified; Star Test Center
Food Facilities: Meals at the cafe; hot snacks and drinks at the
    ski center.
Lodging: Inns and hotels in the area.
How to Get There: I-91 to Brattleboro, Vermont; Route 30
    northwest, then Route 100 north to Londonderry.

Viking is one of the original New England touring centers, dating back more than 15 years now. It has a variety of offerings for skiers of all levels, and like most well-established centers, really emphasizes the proper education of a skier. The trail system is absolutely superb, with intelligently cut and marked trails for every level, and with guided tours out to beautiful remote backlands like Brown Pond in the Green Mountains' Lye Brook Wilderness Area.

Just as it should, the center fixes on skier needs; a complete rental and retail facility is available, along with a wax room and plenty of advice and discussion about the potion of the day. Lodging and expanded dining facilities are available at any number of inns and hotels in the Manchester/Londonderry area.

RABBIT HILL INN

Lower Waterford, Vermont 05848
802-748-5168

Hours: Dawn to dusk.
Trail System: 25 kilometers (about 16 miles).
Trail Difficulty: Easiest, more difficult.
Trail Grooming: Yes.
Rental Equipment: Yes.
Instruction: Limited (call ahead).
Food Facilities: Breakfast and dinner.
Lodging: 20 rooms with private baths; some with working fireplaces.
How to Get There: Route 18 from Littleton, New Hampshire, to St. Johnsbury, Vermont; then 6 miles from the termination of I-93.

Rabbit Hill's trails meander along the Connecticut River, through groves of beechwoods, past beaver lodges, and up Rabbit Hill for a look back over the picturesque village anchored by a white New England meeting house. This is quiet, quality skiing away from the masses. Trails cross much private land, looping through wide meadows that plunge into forested river bank. The 1795 inn with its 20 bedrooms once served 100 horse teams daily that hauled produce from Portland, Maine, to interior New England and Montreal. Nearly all

93

the rooms have mountain views, and the cuisine, enhanced by the inn's own wine cellar, is exquisite. Aside from skiing, the inn provides guided nature walks and climbs in the White Mountains.

FOX RUN RESORT
RFD 1, Box 123
Ludlow, Vermont 05149
802-228-8871

Hours: 8 a.m. to 5 p.m.
Trail System: 30 kilometers (19 miles).
Trail Difficulty: Easiest, more difficult, most difficult.
Trail Grooming: Yes.
Rental Equipment: Yes.
Instruction: PSIA-certified.
Food Facilities: Dining room in a converted barn on the premises.
Lodging: At the Okemo Inn across the street; other areas have bed and breakfast lodging.
How to Get There: Route I-91 to Exit 6, then Route 103 north to Ludlow.

The Fox Run Resort has grown in trail size over the years, so that it now qualifies as a moderately large area with a full-range system through fir-forested terrain that gives skiers some nice views of Okemo Mountain. The trails vary from flat racers to choppy bushwhacking and serious verticals for the expert skier. There is also now a full rental and retail shop available on the premises, as well as certified instructors who will help you bone up on racing technique for Saturday's citizens race, or take you on a guided tour of the network. In the inn, the wood beams glowing with the light from copper lamps make a nice ambiance to loosen down from the day's skiing.

DARION INN SKI TOURING CENTER
Box 173
Lyndonville, Vermont 05851
802-626-5181

Hours: 9 a.m. to 4:30 p.m.
Trail System: 50 kilometers (about 31 miles).
Trail Difficulty: Easiest, more difficult, most difficult.
Trail Grooming: Yes.
Rental Equipment: Yes.
Instruction: Yes.
Food Facilities: Touring center has lunches and trail snacks; full restaurant and bar at the Inn.
Lodging: The inn has 23 rooms; nearby Bunkhouse can accommodate 90.
How to Get There: I-91 to Exit 23 and Lyndonville, Vermont; Route 5 north to Route 114 north to East Burke, then a left turn after the Mobil station; cross the bridge and left at the fork.

With a sweeping view of the Northeast Kingdom—Burke Mountain to the Willoughby Gap—the Darion experience combines the really rugged wildness of the terrain with the opulence of New England country inn living. The inn is really an old estate with a feudal feel as, sitting high on Darling hill, it commands its surroundings. The trails system meanders out over broad meadows and carriage roads around the estate, then plunges through the deep birch and maple forest with ever-apparent wildlife. Encounters with fox and deer are not uncommon in this region. Some trails surge up into the high meadowland with some exciting descents and heart-pumping climbs. One of the best trails runs along parallel to the Passumpsic River, and another runs about 5 kilometers to a wood-stove-warmed sugar house—a fine place to stop for lunch. The area features several citizens' races including a marathon around Presidents' Week. This is excellent skiing for beginners and intermediates, and the real heavy terrain won't disappoint experts.

The center features full retails and rentals, and excellent instruction. Adjoining the center is The Creamery, a restaurant and tavern that makes a wonderful destination for the late afternoon home run.

BIRCH HILL INN
West Road, Box 346
Manchester, Vermont 05254

Hours: Dawn to dusk, as conditions prevail.
Trail System: 13 kilometers (about 8 miles).
Trail Difficulty: Easiest, more difficult, most difficult.
Trail Grooming: None, except for snowmobile tracks.
Rental Equipment: None.
Instruction: None.
Food Facilities: Only for guests of the inn.
Lodging: At the inn.
How to Get There: Route 30 in the center of Manchester north toward Dorset; left onto Manchester West Road, some ¼ mile to Birch Hill Inn.

This area's 8 miles of gladed trails is maintained exclusively for guests of Birch Hill Inn, one of the most postcard-lovely inns in New England. The skiing begins at a small brook-fed pond that gurgles in and out of woods. The trails—of varying degree of difficulty—are picturesque, solitary courses through the quiet Vermont woods. For novices, Birch Hill will send a guide from the inn. On returning, skiers experience the best in New England inn life as proprietor Jim Lee takes you on a tour of the art hangings—many watercolors of skiers. Dinner is a large country affair, as are the breakfasts. Downhill skiing is available nearby at Stratton, Bromley, and Magic.

HILDENE SKI TOURING CENTER
Box 377
Manchester, Vermont 05254
802-362-1788

Hours: 9 a.m. to 5 p.m.
Trail System: 32 kilometers (about 20 miles).
Trail Difficulty: Easiest, more difficult, most difficult.
Trail Grooming: 26 kilometers, groomed and trackset; 6 kilometers wilderness.
Rental Equipment: Yes.
Instruction: Private and group by arrangement during the week, regularly on weekends.
Food Facilities: Hot soups and cocoa during the week; pot-o'soup and chili on weekends.
Lodging: Motels and inns nearby.
How to Get There: Route 30 north to Manchester Center, Vermont; left onto Route 7A.

This historic estate was built by Robert Todd Lincoln, son of President Abraham Lincoln. It is a 412-acre estate with trail meandering about a central warming hut in the old Carriage Barn. New this year: ski rental equipment, one new trail with long downhill runs on a gradual slope, and a potbellied stove. There is something here for the veteran skier as well as the novice, and all phases in between. Special events beyond the skiing are dog sleds, sleigh rides behind a team of Belgian horses, tours of the main house during the Lincoln's birthday holiday period and Christmas.

CARROL AND JANE RIKERT SKI TOURING CENTER
At Breadloaf
Middlebury College Science Building
Middlebury, Vermont 05753
802-388-7947

Hours: 9 a.m. to 5 p.m.
Trail System: 35 kilometers (about 22 miles).
Trail Difficulty: Easiest, more difficult, most difficult.

Trail Grooming: Groomed and double trackset.
Rental Equipment: Yes.
Instruction: Yes.
Food Facilities: Light snacks and hot drinks at the center; restaurant nearby.
Lodging: Hotels and motels in the area, within 13 miles of the touring center.
How to Get There: I-93 to I-89 to Route 100 in Bethel, Vermont; Route 125 east in Hancock.

The annual Middlebury Winter Carnival Nordic events are staged at this highly manicured touring center—an indication of the quality of the trail system and the grooming, marking, and care of the trails. Set in the Breadloaf Campus at Middlebury, the trails course around the Robert Frost Memorial here in the base of the Green Mountains. Some trails run out to the Snow Bowl, and one direction links up with the Blueberry Hill Touring Center trail system. This area is largely for intermediate skiing with some gentle flats available, too. There are waxes available along with rental and retail gear at the center. A warming hut is on the premises.

ALPINE HAVEN
Montgomery Center, Vermont 05471
802-326-4567

Hours: 9 a.m. to 4 p.m.
Trail System: 24 kilometers (15 miles).
Trail Difficulty: Easiest, more difficult, most difficult.
Trail Grooming: Yes, as necessary.
Rental Equipment: No, but nearby.
Instruction: No, but nearby.
Food Facilities: Breakfast, lunch, and dinner available at the hotel.
Lodging: At the Alpine Meadows Hotel, the Hotel Jay, or among the several chalets in the area.
How to Get There: I-91 to Orleans, Vermont, exit; then Route 105 to Route 101 to the Alpine Haven Hotel between Jay Center and Montgomery Center.

To the southwest of Jay Peak, bordering on the immense Northeast Wilderness Kingdom, Alpine Haven offers a landscape of cruising over gentle rollers to the more hilly ruggedness along the side of Jay Peak's Alpine terrain. This is secluded skiing in the true northern wilderness, though Telemarkers who wish to practice have the aerial tram at Jay Peak and some long, smooth runouts down the green-circle Alpine trails.

The Alpine Haven Hotel offers sauna, game room, or just some lounging around the big stone fireplace. The dining room is formal, the food excellent, and the bedrooms large and modern. Nearby, the Hotel Jay has fine accommodations for the destination skier, too. This is a region peopled with many Montrealers, and the whole region has a pleasant international feel.

HAZEN'S NOTCH SKI TOURING CENTER
Route 58
Montgomery Center, Vermont 05471
802-326-4708

Hours: 9 a.m. to 4 p.m.

Trail System: 30 kilometers (about 19 miles) of groomed trails with 75 kilometers of back-country trails.

Trail Difficulty: Easiest, more difficult, most difficult.

Trail Grooming: Groomed and trackset as needed.

Rental Equipment: Yes.

Instruction: Much individual attention for novice skiers; special introductory clinics for Telemark skiing.

Food Facilities: At the ski chalet.

Lodging: Overnight accommodations at the guest house at the ski center; inns and motels within 2 miles.

How to Get There: Route I-91 to White River Junction, Vermont; I-89 to Waterbury, Vermont; Route 100 north to Eden, then Route 118 to Montgomery Center; east on Route 58 to Hazen's.

Nestled high in the wild country and heavy snow belt of the Northeast Kingdom, nearly 100 kilometers of trails wind through a mosaic of deep fir forest and mountain meadow-land. These fields open spectacular views of several mountain ranges, while the backcountry trails lead to little villages and into the dramatic Hazen's Notch. Skiers can find lodging at the center where a guest house offers warm, friendly surroundings that seem a haven after skiing in these winter wilds. After a drink and hot homemade food, high-energy skiers can go back out on guided moonlight tours. Lamps are provided. Telemark clinics and slopes for practice are also available. The Touring Center has a wonderful French/English mix that gives this Green Mountain jewel the kind of international feeling that Alpine skiers find at Jay Peak.

VERMONT VOYAGER EXPEDITIONS
Route 242
Montgomery Center, Vermont 05471
802-326-4789

"VVE," as its students call it, is not a touring area as such but rather a year-round mountaineering school associated with Jay Peak in the Northeast Wilderness Kingdom in the northern part of the state. It also is part of an elaborate inn-to-inn touring system that is part of the Northern Frontier Ski Region of Vermont.

VVE, founded in 1980, is dedicated to "the conservationists of wilderness through the education of its users." VVE has been giving instruction in the practical end of wilderness skiing, giving individuals or groups the confidence to explore this exciting corner of the sport of cross-country. Before skiers can try the wilderness experience, they must learn it, which means it must be taught. That is what VVE is all about. Skiers can use VVE for their destination, then under the tutelege of expert outdoorsmen and guides, undertake as much or as little as they feel up to in this vast unspoiled terrain among the northernmost peaks of the Green Mountains, as well as the lowland trails that lead through meadows and farms and in and out of remote northern villages.

100

THE MONTPELIER ELKS SKI TOURING CENTER
Country Club Road
Montpelier, Vermont 05602
802-229-9409 or 802-223-7457

Hours: Weekends January through March, 9 a.m. to 5 p.m.
Trail System: 8 kilometers (about 5 miles).
Trail Difficulty: Easiest, more difficult.
Trail Grooming: Packed and trackset as needed.
Rental Equipment: Yes.
Instruction: By appointment.
Food Facilities: Full meals at the Montpelier Elks Club.
Lodging: Several hotels and motels nearby.
How to Get There: I-93 to I-89 to Exit 7, Route 302 to Route 2
    east to country club on left. Touring Center is at the top of
    the hill.

This small family-oriented touring center in the Barre/Mont-
pelier region is most suited to day touring, or as an alternative
for Alpine skiers staying in the area. The trails are gently
rolling, open-field loops that won't test the expert, yet can provide plenty of exercise along the golf course terrain. Expan-
sion plans are under way at Montpelier Elks that will double
the ski acreage.

PROSPECT MOUNTAIN SKI TOURING CENTER
34 West Road
Old Bennington, Vermont 05201
802-442-2575

Hours: 9 a.m. to 5 p.m.
Trail System: 25 kilometers (15½ miles).
Trail Difficulty: Easiest, more difficult, most difficult.
Trail Grooming: 15 kilometers groomed and trackset; 10 kilo-
    meters of wilderness terrain.
Rental Equipment: 60 sets.
Instruction: Yes.
Food Facilities: Lunch only served at the base lodge.

Lodging: Greenwood Lodge nearby accommodates groups; motels in the area.

How to Get There: Route 2 to I-91 to Bennington, Vermont; then Route 9 to Wilmington and follow signs to Prospect Mountain.

A high-altitude ski touring center (2,150 feet) in the Green Mountains of western Vermont, Prospect Mountain usually retains a snow cover after the flatlands are bare. The area offers as wide a variety as any ski area in New England—from flat running tracks, to wilderness bushwhacking, to Telemarking on the nearby downhill area, even to guided inn-to-inn ski tours for all levels through the National Forest. Included in the trail fee is a single chairlift ride or unlimited use of the rope tow for skiers who want to practice or take lessons for Telemarking.

Groomed tracks break down to roughly 5 kilometers of most difficult and 10 of more difficult. One loop, the Hawthorne Wilderness Trail that runs off the Mountain Trail to the Danish Delight Wilderness Loop, will give experts all they can handle for twisting, pitching terrain with plenty of up-ing and down-ing. Another wilderness trail, the Beaver Meadow Trail, is merely beautiful as it plunges through the deep woodlands.

WILD WINGS SKI TOURING CENTER
Peru, Vermont 05152
802-824-6793

Hours: 9 a.m. to 4 p.m.

Trail System: 20 kilometers (about 13 miles).

Trail Difficulty: Easiest, more difficult, most difficult.

Trail Grooming: 15 kilometers groomed and trackset as needed.

Rental Equipment: Yes.

Instruction: PSIA-certified.

Food Facilities: Hot drinks and snacks in the warming rooms and at nearby restaurants.

Lodging: Within 3 to 10 miles, tourers can find inns and motels.

How to Get There: I-91 to Brattleboro, Vermont; Route 30 northwest to Route 11, east to Peru; left at the Peru Church and follow to Wild Wings.

Still in the Green Mountains National Forest, this is a small, extremely cozy sort of area out of some of the touring bustle or the hot-shot race crowd in skintight suits. In a converted horse barn you'll find a rental shop and warming/waxing room, then go out skiing over 10 to 12 miles of groomed trails. This system feeds into the vast Green Mountain trail system as well. This home of the wild turkey is one of the prettiest ski regions in New England.

WILDERNESS TRAILS AND NORDIC SKI SCHOOL
c/o The Quechee Inn
Quechee, Vermont 05059
802-295-7620; Off-season, 802-295-3133.

Hours: 9 a.m. to dark.
Trail System: 15 kilometers (about 9 miles).
Trail Difficulty: Easiest, more difficult, most difficult.
Trail Grooming: Machine trackset.
Rental Equipment: Yes.
Instruction: Two PSIA-certified instructors.
Food Facilities: A trailside restaurant, Red Pines, serves hot
   chocolate, coffee, and snacks free when trail pass is
   shown. Breakfast and dinner is available at the inn.
Lodging: 22 units at the inn; other motels nearby.
How to Get There: I-93 north to I-89; at White River Junction,
   Route 4 west toward Woodstock, and signs to Quechee. At
   the sign, right onto Clubhouse Road; 1 mile to the inn.

The touring at Quechee is among the most uniquely beautiful
anywhere, with the most spectacular trail running along the
rim of Quechee Gorge. Here, a waterfall plunges 165 feet down
into the gorge. Skiers are treated to a wildlife area where
sightings of mink, otter, beaver, fox, and porcupines are common. For birders, rare pileated woodpecker is in the trees, as
are owls encountered on moonlight tours. Ask for Marty Ba-
nak for tips on the wildlife tour. Generally Wilderness Trails is
a nice low-key sort of area known mostly for its emphasis on
teaching. In the Woodstock area, there is plenty of skiing (both
Nordic and Alpine) as well as nightlife and shopping in the
region.

GREEN MOUNTAIN TOURING CENTER
At the Three Stallion Inn
Randolph, Vermont 05060
802-728-5575

Hours: Dawn to dusk.
Trail System: 35 kilometers (21 miles).
Trail Difficulty: Easiest, more difficult, most difficult.
Trail Grooming: Daily.
Rental Equipment: Yes.
Instruction: Yes.
Food Facilities: Meals served to guests in the farmhouse.
Lodging: 15 rooms at the farmhouse; other inns and motels in
    the area.
How to Get There: I-93 to I-89 north to Exit 4; then Route 66
    west; left on Stock Farm Road to the touring center.

The Green Mountain Touring Center is one of those no-non-sense, homey resorts that call to skiers who seek the simplicity of a fine trail system, good hot homemade food, and plenty of hospitality in a Victorian farmhouse inn. This center seems to weed out the essential pleasures of the sport from the frills that merely cost money and get in the way. Skiers at Green Mountain will find a big, conscientiously groomed and marked trail system spread out on nearly 1,400 acres of Green Mountain forestland where more than a few U.S. Ski Team members have trained over the years. The terrain rolls along gentle ridges and plunges into woods that can offer skiers any level of vertical ups and downs. For novices there are plenty of flat trails as well. New at the center are a cocktail lounge and restaurant open to the public at lunch and dinner; meals at the inn are for guests, and there is entertainment on weekends. Look into this inn as a four-season destination.

SHERMAN HOLLOW
RFD 1, Box 175
Richmond, Vermont 05477
802-434-2057

Hours: 9 a.m. to 10 p.m.
Trail System: 40 kilometers (25 miles).
Trail Difficulty: Easiest, more difficult, most difficult.
Trail Grooming: 40 kilometers one-way system with double
     trackset; 3.5 kilometers lighted nightly from 6 to 10 p.m.
Rental Equipment: Yes.
Instruction: Yes.
Food Facilities: Yes. Short-order cooking from 9 a.m. to 10
     p.m.; full dining in the evening.
Lodging: At Butternut Lodge or nearby, in Richmond.
How to Get There: I-89 to Exit 11 (Richmond) to Route 2E to
     Sherman Hollow.

The Sherman Hollow Lodge system is one of the more impec-
cably groomed ski terrains we have experienced. Much racing
and race training activity centers there along with the recreational skier of every level. The trails vary from smooth flats to
near-wilderness skiing. Most of the cross-country race practice takes place on the groomed portion. From the fast track,
however, there is touring out to the Butternut Lodge area with
its views of the dramatic Camel's Hump—Vermont's Motif
Number One. After the trek out through the fine trail system,
weary skiers can plump into the outdoor hot tub at the lodge
while enjoying a selection from the Eight Pointer Lounge. Under construction is a village complex with a 70-room inn, indoor sports center, conference center, rental shops, 72
condominium units, a theater, and outdoor amphitheater. Also
in the works is an 18-hole golf course.

NORDIC ADVENTURES
Dean Mendell
Box 155, RFD 1
Rochester, Vermont 05767
802-767-3996

Hours: 8 a.m. to dark.
Trail System: Any and all accessible lands can be used.
Trail Difficulty: Easiest, more difficult.
Trail Grooming: Foot-packed or groomed with snowmobile.
Rental Equipment: 20 sets of waxable back-country skis.
Instruction: PSIA-certified instructor.
Food Facilities: A country lunch is offered on guided tours.
Lodging: Inns at the area.
How to Get There: I-93 to I-89 north to the exit at Bethel,
    Vermont; then Route 107 to Route 100 north. Mendell's
    house is 4 miles south of Rochester Village on Route 100
    North.

Nordic Adventures is an outfitter and guide system that offers
more personalized instruction on a one-to-one basis. Skiers
interested in back-country forays have a choice of several
package plans, including inn-to-inn ski hikes, Norpine instruction, and moonlight escapades. A typical five-day package in
the $350 range would include lodging costs, all meals and
guide and instruction fees, luggage transfer, taxes, and gratui-
ties. This is a different approach to touring than the ordinary
destination trip, and should appeal to skiers who really like to
probe into the woolly corners of the sport. Mr. Mendell knows
the woods, and can personally arrange a wilderness tour to fit
individual skiers' tastes and abilities.

KEDRON VALLEY INN
Route 106, Box 145
South Woodstock, Vermont 05071
802-457-1473

Hours: Dawn to dusk.
Trail System: 20 kilometers (about 12 miles).
Trail Difficulty: More difficult, most difficult.
Trail Grooming: Snowmobile trackset.
Rental Equipment: Yes.
Instruction: Some, but limited.
Food Facilities: Three meals daily at the inn.
Lodging: 31 rooms at the inn and motel.
How to Get There: I-93 to I-89 north to Exit 1; Route 4 to
    Woodstock; Route 106 south to the inn.

Hardly an elaborate touring center, The Kedron Valley Inn, dating to 1828, is nevertheless a prime example of Vermont country-inn living. In 1968 a tastefully designed log motel was built on the site as well, and for years this area, nestled in the Green Mountains, catered to horseback riders and all sorts of summer vacationers. But when the snow is prime, so is the touring through woods, frozen stream beds, and along groomed tracks around the inn. Three accomplished skiers at the inn offer guide services and instruction. Barbara and Paul Kendrall, descendants of the original settlers here 200 years ago, run the inn with its big fireplaced living rooms, simple home-style cuisine, and the excellent Tavern lounge for skiers looking for some day's-end refreshment. For variation, the nearby town of Woodstock has quality shopping, sightseeing, and restaurants. Downhill skiing is nearby at Suicide Six; Killington is 45 minutes away.

TRAIL HEAD SKI TOURING
Star Route
Stockbridge, Vermont 05772
802-746-8038

*We liked this
one the best
Nice family owned/run
place*

Hours: 9 a.m. to 5 p.m.
Trail System: 45 kilometers (about 28 miles).
Trail Difficulty: Easiest, more difficult, most difficult.
Trail Grooming: Partially; machine-set on beginner to intermediate terrain; most of the expert trails foot-packed.
Rental Equipment: Yes.
Instruction: Yes.
Food Facilities: Homemade soups, snacks, drinks, and sandwiches in the lodge. Restaurants in the area for dinners.
Lodging: Seven lodging establishments within five minutes of the area.
How to Get There: I-93 to I-89 to Route 107 in Vermont; then to Route 100 south for 1 mile to the touring center.

Near Rutland, Vermont, the Trail Head Touring Center is a large system in the Green Mountain National Forest offering a variety of touring experiences. Skiers can warm up with open-meadow cruising over well-set tracks, then roll down along the lovely Tweed River trails that course in and out of deep woods. More advanced skiers have the option of some real pumping terrain along the South Hill or out to the Liberty Hill System. Most of the ski terrain offers some nice glimpses of the nearby Alpine terrain. Back at the lodge, a converted barn from the 1870s, cold, tired skiers lounge in front of the roaring fire sipping drinks and homemade soups. Here they find a complete rental and retail facility, and can sign up for lessons and PSIA-certified instructors or citizens races. Also available are moonlit excursions through the river valley and over the pastureland. With Killington Ski Area nearby, there is plenty of nightlife for the indefatigable skier, as well as good lodging and dining. Trail Head is an excellent day- or destination-trip for skiers of every level.

EDSON HILL MANOR
Edson Hill Road
Stowe, Vermont 05672
802-253-7371

Hours: 9 a.m. to 5 p.m.
Trail System: 95 kilometers (about 59 miles).
Trail Difficulty: Easiest, more difficult, most difficult.
Trail Grooming: Daily, as needed.
Rental Equipment: Yes.
Instruction: Yes.
Food Facilities: At the Manor house.
Lodging: Rooms of two to three bedrooms at the Manor house.
How to Get There: I-91 to I-89 northwest to Exit 10; Route 100
    north to Stowe Village; Route 108 west; take the right fork
    on Edson Hill Road to the manor.

This rather overlooked, under-publicized area has a mammoth
trail system, few crowded days, and gorgeous terrain for first-
out novices and old hands alike. The trails, spread out over a
400-acre estate, are contained in fair flat, gladed meadowland.
Then the fun begins, as skiers climb off the flats, if they wish,
into some backland touring in the rugged Green Mountain
terrain. The wax shop is complete, and has a nice feel of the
horse barn that it serves as in the warm season. Here skiers
can obtain retail gear of all kinds, rent skis, try to get words of
free advice from the experts all around, or put down a little
cash for a real lesson. The Edson Hill Manor itself is not quite
in the character of the old Vermont inn tour, yet is extremely
relaxing, gentle, and stress removing. The food is fine, the
atmosphere bright and supple. Also available to skiers is a
country inn.

MT. MANSFIELD SKI TOURING CENTER
Mountain Road
Stowe, Vermont 05672
802-253-7311

Hours: 9 a.m. to 4 p.m.
Trail System: 50 kilometers (about 31 miles).
Trail Difficulty: Easiest, more difficult, most difficult.
Trail Grooming: Double trackset on 25 kilometers.
Rental Equipment: Yes.
Instruction: Yes.
Food Facilities: Full-service restaurant at the base lodge, and several restaurants on the road between Mansfield and Stowe.
Lodging: At the Inn at the Mountain.
How to Get There: Route I-89 to Exit 10; then 10 miles north on Route 100 to Stowe Village; left on Route 108 for 5 miles.

Always noted as one of the ski capitals of the East, Stowe's 50 kilometers of mapped Nordic trails (25 kilometers are groomed and trackset) live up to that reputation. Mt. Mansfield offers a variety of terrain for every ability level in acreage that plunges deep into the solitude and beauty of the Green Mountains. Intersecting with other trail systems, skiers from Mt. Mansfield actually have 150 kilometers of trails at their disposal.

Using both sides of the historic Ranch Valley up the flanks of Mt. Mansfield, these trails are exceptionally well maintained, a complex that provides the basis for the famous Stowe Derby—an annual 12-mile trot from the top of Mansfield into the village of Stowe. Two wilderness trails connect with the Skytop Trail and the luncheon cabin of the Trapp Family Lodge complex, allowing a full day of touring or wilderness exploration.

TOPNOTCH TOURING CENTER
Mountain Road
Stowe, Vermont 05672
802-253-8585

Hours: 9 a.m. to 5 p.m.
Trail System: 90 kilometers (about 56 miles).
Trail Difficulty: Easiest, more difficult, most difficult.
Trail Grooming: 20 kilometers groomed daily.
Rental Equipment: Yes.
Instruction: Yes.
Food Facilities: The entire Stowe area is a culinary delight.
Lodging: Dozens of inns and motels in the town of Stowe.
How to Get There: I-89 to Route 100 north; then Route 108
    northwest. Topnotch is between Stowe Village and Mount
    Mansfield.

Like all ski centers of this region, the town of Stowe itself is
the draw here for the destination skier. Our advice is to book
trips well ahead, especially in busy seasons. The inn itself
features lodging toward the luxury end of the spectrum, and
dining to match in this very competitive restaurant area. The
trail system, though it does offer some trails in the "most
difficult" category, is geared toward less stressful skiing. The
Lower and Upper Valley Trails send skiers over some rugged
terrain that eventually makes a link with Trapp Lodge's trail
system. Another route along some much easier terrain ties
skiers in with the Edson Hill Manor trails. Yet another route
(Cross Cut) winds skiers into the Mt. Mansfield downhill area
for some Telemark practice. For the less adventurous, the
trails close to the Topnotch Center itself are nicely groomed,
gentle rollers that run along open meadows, through woodland, and along the West Branch River. Topnotch is an excellent spot for both the casual and the more serious skier.

TRAPP FAMILY LODGE
Stowe, Vermont 05672
802-253-8511

Hours: 9 a.m. to 5 p.m.
Trail System: About 96 kilometers (60 miles).
Trail Difficulty: Easiest, more difficult, most difficult.
Trail Grooming: Groomed and trackset.
Rental Equipment: 400 sets.
Instruction: PSIA-certified.
Food Facilities: Restaurant and lounge; lunches served at cabin or on the trail system.
Lodging: 73 rooms on premises.
How to Get There: I-91 (or I-93) to I-89, northwest to Exit 10; Route 100 north to Stowe.

The famous Trapp Family Lodge is still credited as the origin of Nordic skiing in America. Its fabled setting—and historical background—makes it certainly the best-known touring capital in the East, and perhaps the best commercial touring operation in the country.

The well-groomed and -marked trail system stretches out over 1,700 acres of Green Mountain terrain, and offers diversity that ranges from open golf course terrain to wooded thickets to real wilderness skiing where it borders on the limitless. Obviously, there is a wide variety of skill levels offered here, and the Trapps provide excellent private or group skiing lessons. The site of many collegiate and world class races, the lodge also offers racing seminars and back-country tours.

While there is lodging at the Trapp Family Lodge, it is usually booked months in advance, but there is plenty of lodging throughout Stowe village, along with some extremely precious nightlife.

STRATTON MOUNTAIN SKI TOURING CENTER
Stratton Mountain, Vermont 05155
802-297-1880 or 802-297-2200, Extension 2222.

Hours: 8:30 a.m. to 4 p.m.
Trail System: 20 kilometers (about 13 miles).
Trail Difficulty: Easiest, most difficult.
Trail Grooming: Daily.
Rental Equipment: 175 sets.
Instruction: Yes.
Food Facilities: Meals served 1½ miles from the center at the Cub's Pub dining room.
Lodging: Inns and motels available; call the Stratton reservation service at 802-222-1300.
How to Get There: I-91 to Brattleboro, Vermont; Route 30 northwest to Bondville, then left onto the Stratton Mountain access road.

Ski touring at Stratton is like most other things at Stratton—like the Alpine skiing, golf, or tennis. In a word, classy. Stratton is a smooth operation where skiers tour on a smooth and rolling golf course and along wooded trails with pretty views of Stratton Mountain itself, Bromley, and Magic Mountains. The meandering trails roll through the foothills of the Alpine slopes, some groomed with some others left open.

Stratton's center grooms and tracks 13 miles of trails which take skiers through a variety of experiences, from flat-track running to big rolling heart-stoppers. There are some excellent wilderness trails on the National Forest Terrain—all free. All the rest of Stratton is excellent skiing, well marked, and leading to a finely appointed lodge for fire, food, drink, and plenty of talk about the wax you should have used. There are good snacks at the center. Every Saturday night there is a guided tour of Stratton Pond, and in February there is a cross-country ski festival with plenty of factory vendors and ski reps.

TUCKER HILL SKI TOURING CENTER
Tucker Hill Lodge
RFD 1, Box 147
Waitsfield, Vermont 05673
802-496-3203 (Lodge, 802-496-3983; toll free 800-451-4580)

Hours: 9 a.m. to 5 p.m.
Trail System: 45 kilometers, plus back-country trails.
Trail Difficulty: Easiest, more difficult, most difficult.
Trail Grooming: Yes, regularly.
Rental Equipment: Skis, including Telemark; snowshoes.
Instruction: PSIA-certified.
Food Facilities: Breakfast and dinner at Tucker Hill Lodge.
   Lunch at the touring center.
Lodging: 20 rooms at the Tucker Hill Lodge; also available at
   Plum Creek.
How to Get There: I-93 to I-89 to Route 100 south to Waitsfield;
   then Route 17 west to Tucker Hill Lodge.

The Tucker Hill Center is connected to the Sugarbush/Rossignol Ski Touring Center and also the Mad River Nordic Center. The cooperative effort of these areas does much to promote ski touring at a high level; a five-day pass can be obtained to cover the four centers. This southern Vermont area has an extensive, varied and well-groomed trail network with an emphasis on wooded terrain geared mostly toward the intermediate skier. There's not much here to curl the toes, nor is there much flat-track open terrain for beginners. The trails run over ancient logging roads, and one route leads to the woods-bound Plum Creek, where skiers can find a hot meal and spend the night. The area is also active in citizens racing, provides clinics on technique and waxing, and stages a Triathlon in March, attracting from 400 to 500 skiers who actually undertake four events: skiing, canoeing, running, and bicycling. Not for everyone, perhaps, but fun to see.

OLE'S CROSS COUNTRY
Airport Road
Warren, Vermont 08674
800-496-3430

Hours: 9 a.m. to 5 p.m.
Trail System: 40 kilometers (about 27 miles).
Trail Difficulty: Easiest, more difficult, most difficult.
Trail Grooming: More than 20 kilometers.
Rental Equipment: Yes.
Instruction: Group and private.
Food Facilities: Cafeteria has hot soups and sandwiches.
Lodging: Nearby.
How to Get There: I-89 north to Exit 3; Route 107 south to
    Route 100, then north to Warren; right on Brook Road,
    then left onto Roxbury Gap Road, then left again into
    Ole's.

When the Warren-Sugarbush Airport closes for the winter,
that's when Ole Mosesen, a fishing guide from Norway, begins
setting tracks throughout the airport terrain—fields and gen-
tle-to-tough woodlands—and gets out the wax to teach novices
what they're about. After his waxing clinics—occasionally in-
volving U.S. Ski Team members—Ole serves hot lunch to skiers at his cafe. The trail system here is a scenic network
through the Mad River Valley with six interconnecting trail
loops that range from a 2-mile exercise loop to some heavily
pitched verticals for the tough runners. One trail, a 16-kilome-
ter bash through the woods, known as Holly King trail, will
leave the most seasoned tourer both exhilarated and beat. Beyond this for the real experts is Scrag Mountain. Full retail
and rentals are available.

SUGARBUSH INN/ROSSIGNOL SKI TOURING CENTER
Access Road
Warren, Vermont 05674
802-583-2301

Hours: 9 a.m. to 5 p.m.
Trail System: 50 kilometers (about 31 miles).
Trail Difficulty: Easiest, more difficult, most difficult.
Trail Grooming: Groomed and double trackset daily.
Rental Equipment: Yes.
Instruction: Yes.
Food Facilities: Across the street from the touring center at the
    Sugarbush Inn.
Lodging: The inn has 46 rooms.
How to Get There: I-93 to I-89 north to Exit 9 at Warren/Waits-
    field, Vermont; Route 100 to Warren, then left onto the
    Sugarbush Valley Access Road; the center is 2 miles on
    the left.

Located in the skirts of the Green Mountains, the Sugarbush/
Rossignol center is a complete, expertly operated and maintained cross-country facility that appeals equally to the racing
expert and the recreational skiing family. The center offers 35
kilometers of meticulously groomed and marked trails that
vary the experience greatly. There is the 15-kilometer racing
trail, for example, that cranks you quickly skyward through
twisting mountain trails. Or you can choose the open-field
skiing along the flats of the golf course, or the long, fairly
gentle wooded run along German Flats Road to the Tucker
Hill Touring Center.

At the touring center, you can sign up for lessons at any
level, as well as racing clinics. The center can even arrange a
demonstration ride on some Rossignol racing skis for those
who want to pursue the go-fast end of the sport, and perhaps a
citizens race. With the proximity of the Sugarbush Alpine
area, the ski school will also help you work on your Telemark
technique. The center has a full retail/rental facility and waxing rooms. Moonlight tours are available through the season.

TIMBER CREEK SKI TOURING CENTER
Box 860
West Dover, Vermont 05356
802-464-2323

Hours: 8:30 a.m. to 4:30 p.m.
Trail System: 5 kilometers.
Trail Difficulty: Easiest, more difficult, most difficult.
Trail Grooming: Groomed and trackset.
Rental Equipment: Yes.
Instruction: PSIA-certified.
Food Facilities: Restaurant within 1 mile. Light snacks and drinks at the center.
Lodging: Condominiums at Timber Creek; motels and hotels in the area.
How to Get There: I-91 to Route 9 west to Brattleboro; west for 20 miles to Wilmington, Vermont; Route 100 for 8 miles to Mt. Snow entrance; touring center is across the street.

This new ski-touring center across from Mt. Snow, with its panoramic view toward Wilmington valley, provides for all skiers' needs and desires. The touring varies from old logging trails across rolling terrain, to open flats and manicured tracks, to skiing in the woolly wilderness of these parts. There are frozen streams and rivers in the woods, deep pine groves and stands of hardwood. There is a warming hut out on the trails. Timber Creek may be small, but it is expanding in its trail system size. The center has a full retail and rental operation with a big waxing room. Skiers who want to try some Telemark turning, or simply Alpine skiing, can take a free shuttle across to Mt. Snow.

WINDHAM HILL INN & TOURING CENTER
West Townshend, Vermont 05359
802-874-4080

Hours: Dawn to dusk.
Trail System: 5 kilometers (about 3 miles) of tracked skiing; unlimited wilderness skiing.

119

Trail Difficulty: Easiest, more difficult.
Trail Grooming: Yes, packed.
Rental Equipment: Yes; available free for guests.
Instruction: Yes.
Food Facilities: Meal service for guests of the inn.
Lodging: 15 guest rooms with private baths.
How to Get There: I-91 to Exit 2 and Brattleboro, Vermont; Route 30 north for 22 miles to West Townshend and Windham Hill.

This nineteenth-century restored family farmhouse in southern Vermont is a lovely setting for destination skiers who like primarily wilderness skiing over meadows and through woods. The inn itself, run by Linda and Ken Busteed, offers full amenities for most skiers' tastes, and more: It is rich in antiques and oriental rugs, handmade quilts and original paintings, the charms of a past age. The skiing facility is for the exclusive use of guests. There are no trail fees nor any charge for equipment use. Aside from its own small groomed network, Windham Hill has wild open lands, mostly of the gentle-contour variety. This skiing feeds onto other trail systems like Tater Hill, Viking, Stratton, and Wild Wings.

CATAMOUNT FAMILY CENTER
449 Governŏr Chittenden Road
Williston, Vermont 05495
802-879-6001

Hours: Sunday, Monday, and Tuesday, 9 a.m. to dusk; Wednesday through Saturday, 9 a.m. to 9 p.m.
Trail System: 40 kilometers (about 25 miles).
Trail Difficulty: Easiest, more difficult, most difficult.
Trail Grooming: More than 30 kilometers as needed.
Rental Equipment: 70 sets.
Instruction: PSIA-certified.
Food Facilities: Hot drinks and trail snacks at the center; restaurants available within 3 miles.
Lodging: Bed and breakfast inns and hotels within 2 miles; Burlington, Vermont, is 8 miles away.

How to Get There: I-93 to I-89 to Vermont Exit 12, then north;
   right at the second traffic light; 4 miles to the center.

This fifth-generation family farm outside Burlington typifies
the kind of old-world solid roots at the center of much of
Vermont's charm. The well-groomed and -marked trail system
makes gentle loops over fields and woods in the Champlain
Valley, and offers wonderful sudden views of Camel's Hump
and Mt. Mansfield. Though the grade varies just 300 feet verti-
cally throughout the network, there are still a few huff-and-
puffers like Ridge Run and Skidway that throw you twisting
quick descents. There are heated trail shelters out on the loop.
Catamount's center is a big log cabin with roaring fire, fine
home-cooked food, and all retail and rental needs. At night, 3
kilometers are lit for running.

HERMITAGE CROSS-COUNTRY TOURING CENTER
Coldbrook Road
Wilmington, Vermont 05363
802-464-3511

Hours: 9 a.m. to 4 p.m.
Trail System: 50 kilometers (31 miles).
Trail Difficulty: Easiest, more difficult, most difficult. Tele-
   mark trails.
Trail Grooming: Most trails.
Rental Equipment: Yes.
Instruction: Yes.
Food Facilities: Full meals and trail snacks.
Lodging: At the inn.
How to Get There: I-91 to Brattleboro, Vermont; west on Route
   9 to Wilmington.

Two-thousand feet up in the Vermont sky, The Hermitage has
plenty of snow and touring generally in woods and stream
beds sheltered from the wind. The Ridge Trails run from the
top of Haystack Ski Area to the top of Mt. Snow, a 5-mile trek
through the National Forest. This is a special springtime challenge for expert skiers, and must be guided. In March there

are several challenge races at the area as well. There is also good beginner skiing along the flat floor of the Mt. Snow Valley, and intermediates can climb up along the shoulders of the mountains. Like so many Vermont inns, the Hermitage is reconstructed from an eighteenth-century farmhouse, and offers the kind of quaint charm tourers look for in such places. The 50 kilometers of marked and groomed trails circle from a warming hut, out to Mt. Snow. The touring center offers full retail and rental services, and trail snacks including wine and cheese.

ON THE ROCKS LODGE
Smith Road
Wilmington, Vermont 05363
802-464-8364

Hours: Daylight.

Trail System: On the Rocks Lodge is tied in with the Sitzmark Ski Touring Center with its 25 kilometers of trails. Total network is 40 kilometers (about 26 miles).

Trail Difficulty: More difficult.

Trail Grooming: Packed and trackset regularly.

Rental Equipment: Nearby.

Instruction: Nearby.

Food Facilities: Gourmet cuisine for lodge guests and by reservation; full bar and lounge facility for skiers.

Lodging: Contemporary rooms with private baths available.

How to Get There: I-91 from Brattleboro, Vermont; Route 9 west to Wilmington; then Route 100 north for 4 miles to the town center.

On the Rocks is a small inn straight out of a romantic novel. It sets nearly 2000 feet up in the southern Green Mountains with some terrific views of this rolling range, and of peaks like Mt. Snow and Haystack. These latter locations are full-blown Alpine areas. Cross-country skiers have 40 miles of private trails at their disposal, all of them starting at the door of the inn.

There are plenty of flats for beginners to get their ski legs, and the well seasoned to do some warm-up runs before plunging into the special Wilderness trail that runs through snow-coated woodlands, cellar holes filled with rich history, ponds with beaver lodges and other wildlife—even some beech trees with bear claw marks scratched in the side. If, after the long wilderness tour or the run through the flattish meadows, skiers have anything left in them, the area is near the rollicking Mt. Snow with its celebrated nightlife. This can be embraced or avoided, as skiers wish.

SITZMARK LODGE
Wilmington, Vermont 05363
802-464-8187

Hours: 9 a.m. to 5 p.m.
Trail System: 25 kilometers (about 16 miles).
Trail Difficulty: Easiest, more difficult, most difficult.
Trail Grooming: Trackset daily.
Rental Equipment: Yes.
Instruction: PSIA-certified.
Food Facilities: Meals served at The Barn Lounge.
Lodging: Inns and hotels in the area.
How to Get There: I-91 to Brattleboro, Vermont; Route 9 west
    to Wilmington.

Cross-country skiers at Sitzmark enjoy some spectacular views of the Mt. Snow and Haystack mountain range to the west of the center, as they glide over a wide variety of trails. From the slow rollers, to choppers like Maple Chute and Ponderosa View, this trail system offers something to all levels. There is one 8-mile loop that bears the skier out on a splendid tour to West Dover Inn (1846) for hot drinks and a midday meal. Advanced skiers can climb into some stunning mountain plateaus surrounding the center, while novice skiers get their training on an 18-hole golf course and attendant pasture trails.

New this year, skiers can start their trek at two nearby sites—at Le Petit Chef to ski the Deerfield Pasture or Poplar View Pond. Or, you can try to master the Smith Road. Or, from

Flaim's Farm House, skiers can try the Farm House Loop or stretch out to the Ponderosa View. A valid trail pass from Sitzmark is necessary for these alternative origin points.

THE WHITE HOUSE TOURING CENTER
Route 9
Wilmington, Vermont 05363
802-464-2136

Hours: 9 a.m. to 4:30 p.m.
Trail System: 22 kilometers (about 13 miles).
Trail Difficulty: Easiest, more difficult, most difficult.
Trail Grooming: Consistently over 15 kilometers.
Rental Equipment: 80 sets.
Instruction: Group, three times daily on weekends; 11 a.m. weekdays; video lessons available.
Food Facilities: Continental dining at the White House plus skiers' lunches on weekends.
Lodging: 12 rooms at the White House.
How to Get There: I-91 to Brattleboro, Vermont; Route 9 west to Wilmington and junction of Route 100.

The White House itself, set in the Mt. Snow region, is a turn-of-the-century farm mansion steeped in Vermont's rural hospitality. With full health spa, sauna, steam room, and indoor pool available, and truly exquisite continental cuisine served before roaring fires, this is a place to come home to after a day on the trail. Eight rooms are in the main inn and four are in the north wing.

The trails are skewed toward intermediates, but there is plenty for the novice and expert as well. Skiing begins with undulating meadow skiing over nicely groomed tracks, and progresses to toe-curling downhills over the twisting Raponda Primitive Trail. Not for everyone, this is nevertheless a special run feeding into the Ridge Trail that goes between Haystack and Mt. Snow, and offering wonderful vistas of each. Also available are guided nature tours to search for bear tracks and the like, along with some full moonlight touring. Special weekly discounts are available for senior citizen groups.

HILLTOP CROSS-COUNTRY CENTER
Box 2820
Wolcott, Vermont 05680
802-888-3710

Hours: Saturdays, Sundays, and holidays from 9 a.m. to 5 p.m.
Trail System: 20 kilometers (about 12 miles).
Trail Difficulty: Easiest, more difficult, most difficult.
Trail Grooming: Yes.
Rental Equipment: Yes.
Instruction: No.
Food Facilities: None at the center; restaurant within 3 miles.
Lodging: Within 5 miles.
How to Get There: Route I-93 to I-89 to Route 15.

This small area north of Stowe Village offers good skiing, mostly of the gentle meadow variety, though there is one cranker that sends skiers twisting up and down through the woods. It is very much a locals-area or perhaps a day trip off the beaten path for visitors at Stowe who want to escape the crush for a day. Though the facilities are not for most destination skiers, this is still the luscious land area of northern Vermont, and the trails are an excellent variety of old logging roads and open flats.

WOODSTOCK SKI TOURING CENTER
At the Woodstock Country Club
Route 106
Woodstock, Vermont 05091
802-457-2114

Hours: 9 a.m. to dusk.
Trail System: 75 kilometers (about 47 miles).
Trail Difficulty: Least difficult, more difficult, most difficult.
Trail Grooming: 35 kilometers groomed and double-trackset
    daily.
Rental Equipment: Yes.
Instruction: PSIA-certified.

Food Facilities: Restaurant and bar at the center and at the
Woodstock Inn.
Lodging: Inns and motels in the region.
How to Get There: I-91 to I-89; west to Route 4; west to Route
106; then south to the touring center.

In the heart of this most tweedy Rock Resort (for owner
Laurence Rockefeller) town of Woodstock, Vermont—where
skiing all got organized in America some five decades ago under the agreeable patriarchy of Dartmouth College—this touring area offers an extensive trail system to skiers who can do
without roughing it or the "wilderness experience." It is
rather tuned to those vacationers seeking the pleasures of ski
touring within the resort experience. Woodstock itself, with
the famous inn at its center, is considered by many one of the
loveliest towns in New England.

That said, it is possible for the serious tourer to take off
from the touring center on a 10-mile trek, Skyline Drive—the

oldest trail in the nation cut specifically for cross-country touring. This deposits skiers in the town of East Barnard. Of the 75 kilometers of mapped trails, 35 are trackset and groomed daily. Twenty kilometers are on the fir-laced Mt. Tom, and another 20 wind round Mt. Peg. There are also golf-course skiing, a race loop, and nature trails of varied lengths.

The Touring Center offers one of the most extensive base facilities in New England. It is wonderfully large and replete with a big, steamy shower room, rental shop, ski shop, restaurant, fireplaced lounge, and a large waxing porch. For skiers in fear of overexpending their energy, there is one trail loop that brings you mercifully close to the back door of the Woodstock Inn. Here, for a mere pittance, you can park your skis and start a hot and huge brunch with salmon bisque against a background of Mozart études.

NEW HAMPSHIRE

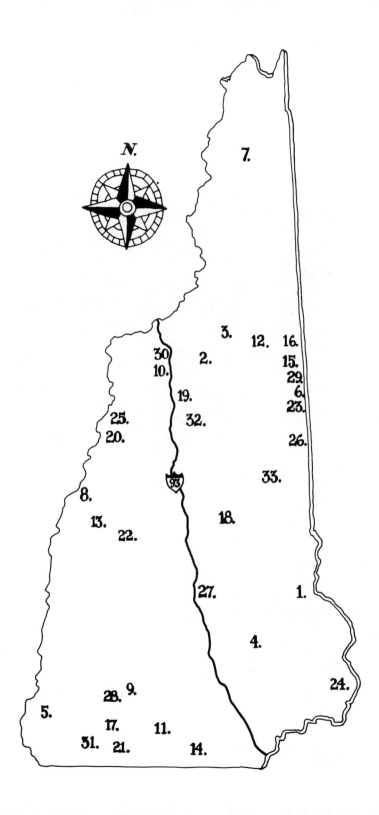

New Hampshire

Numbers on map refer to towns numbered below

NIPPO LAKE TOURING CENTER
Province Road
Barrington, New Hampshire 03825
603-664-2030

Hours: 9 a.m. to dusk.
Trail System: 15 kilometers (about 10 miles).
Trail Difficulty: Easiest, more difficult, most difficult.
Trail Grooming: Regularly groomed and trackset.
Rental Equipment: Yes.
Instruction: None.
Food Facilities: Full restaurant and lounge in the center.
Lodging: Motels in Rochester, about 10 miles distant.
How to Get There: I-95 north to Spaulding Turnpike to Exit 13;
    Route 202 north to Barrington, then Route 126 to Nippo
    Lake Golf Club.

Overlooking the Blue Job Mountain Range, this touring center combines mostly gentle flats skiing with some fairly challenging descents to and around Nippo Lake. The wooded trails, varying from flat to gently rolling to steep, all abound in wildlife—fox, deer, and birds of all kinds. The center has rentals and retail, good food, and a room to wax your skis.

CAMP ALLEN
RFD 5
Bedford, New Hampshire 03102
603-622-8471

Hours: Variable; call ahead.
Trail System: 10 kilometers (about 6 miles).
Trail Difficulty: Easiest, more difficult.
Trail Grooming: Daily.
Rental Equipment: Yes, with advance notice.
Instruction: Yes.
Food Facilities: Snack bar on premises for light lunches.
Lodging: Cabins and other camp buildings.

How to Get There: I-93 to Manchester, New Hampshire; Route
101 west to Route 3; south to a right turn at the Texaco
Station, then less than 2 miles to Camp Allen.

Daily cross-country skiers from the southern tier find Camp
Allen's 70 acres a delightfully convenient area to practice,
work out, or just to meander through nice hardwood forest
solitude only one hour from Boston. Aside from day-trippers,
dormitory facilities are available to accommodate groups of
twenty or less. An indoor fireside area is available for waxing
and relaxing; some retail equipment and rentals are at hand.
Call ahead.

BRETTON WOODS SKI TOURING CENTER
Bretton Woods, New Hampshire
603-278-5181

Hours: 8:30 a.m. to 4:30 p.m.
Trail System: 100 kilometers (about 62 miles).
Trail Difficulty: Least difficult, more difficult, most difficult.
Trail Grooming: Daily maintenance; double trackset on all
trails.
Rental Equipment: Yes.
Instruction: PSIA-certified.
Food Facilities: Food and drink available at the Touring Center
cafeteria, at the Alpine baselodge, Darby's Tavern, and
Fabyan's.
Lodging: At the Bretton Woods Lodge or Rosebrook Town-
houses near the Touring Center.
How to Get There: I-93 to Lincoln, New Hampshire; Route 3
north; turn right on Route 302 to Bretton Woods.

Coursing through the western valley of Mt. Washington, this
spectacular, 100-kilometer trail system is truly all things for
all skiers, from the raw neophyte seeking a leisurely walk
through the White Mountain National Forest, to the serious
racer looking to train on tracks graced in the past by such
world-class runners as Bill Koch, Tim and Jennifer Caldwell,

and Beth Paxson. The U.S Team held its 1982 Nationals here, and the area hosts an annual stop on the Great American Ski Chase marathon series.

Do not be scared off by all this heaviness, however. Bretton Woods' bread and butter is still the casual touring skier, and the area gears itself to just that. A very well-marked trail system offers courses of various lengths and degrees of difficulty, from the broad flats of the golf course on which is located that gorgeous antique, the Mt. Washington Hotel, to the Coronary Hill system which winds into foothills of the Presidential Range. There are three separate but interlocking trail systems at Bretton Woods—the Ammonoosuc, Deception (for Mount Deception), and Stickney, the latter incorporating the Alpine area and offering the most hilly and tough terrain. You'll do well to stay away from the Cog Railway Road since this is a major snowmobile route.

Bretton Woods has lately moved its touring center into a much larger building with full and very well-appointed accommodations—a large restaurant and waxing room, a full rental operation, ski school, and some just-hanging-around space to let skiers thaw the ice out of their beards.

Though skiers can jump on to trails from the roadside anywhere around the White Mountain National Forest here, this is not advised for folks unfamiliar with the area. It is vast. The trail system is bewildering. Part of the trail fee pays for the plasticized maps you pick up at the touring center that offer advice about shelters along the trail, and the level of difficulty for the various routes. The area is on the opposite side of Mt. Washington from Jackson, and as the sun sets on a winter afternoon, the mountain holds the light longer in the sky as it blinks through the spectrum—orange to red to violet to blue. If Jackson is the place to watch the winter sunrise, then Bretton Woods is your spot to view amazing sunsets. Overnight and moonlight excursions are available.

The area has a limited number of beds at this point—less than 100—including existing Rosebrook townhouses and The Lodge motel, but motels are available down Route 302 toward Twin Mountain. Grand plans include more beds to be built on-site in the next year.

CHARMINGFARE SKI TOURING CENTER
Box 146
Candia, New Hampshire 03034
603-483-2307

Hours: 9 a.m. to 4 p.m.
Trail System: 32 kilometers (about 20 miles).
Trail Difficulty: Easiest, more difficult.
Trail Grooming: Groomed and trackset regularly.
Rental Equipment: 200 sets.
Instruction: By appointment on weekends.
Food Facilities: Weekends only, a snack bar and lounge serves
    breakfast and lunch.
Lodging: Inns and motels in Manchester, about 15 miles dis-
    tant.
How to Get There: I-93 to New Hampshire Exit 7; Route 101
    east for 7 miles to a left turn on South Road.

Charmingfare is a golf course within easy reach of the Manchester area, and features gentle skiing for beginners with
plenty of quick running for those with some miles under their
skis. Skiers do not use the course itself, but rather cruise on
trails and railroad beds that roll over broad meadows then
plunge into the hardwood forest; some of these wind along a
high ridge from which, in openings, skiers can overlook lakes
back in the region of Auburn, Massachusetts. The trails at
Charmingfare are loaded with wildlife—beaver ponds and one
rookery of great blue heron. The center offers full rental and
retail at the pro shop, with trail snacks available, and plenty of
indoor space for waxing.

ROAD'S END FARM
Jackson Hill Road
Chesterfield, New Hampshire 03443
603-363-4703

Hours: 9 a.m. to 5 p.m.
Trail System: 30 kilometers (about 18 miles).
Trail Difficulty: Easiest, more difficult, most difficult.

Trail Grooming: As needed.
Rental Equipment: Yes.
Instruction: Weekends, holidays, and school vacations.
Food Facilities: Sandwiches, soup, and snacks available on
    weekends, holidays, and vacations.
Lodging: Inns and motels in the area, and at the farm.
How to Get There: I-91 north to Exit 3 at Brattleboro, Vermont;
    then Route 9E to junction of Route 63; south on Route 63
    to center of Chesterfield; turn left for 1 mile to Jackson
    Hill Road; follow to the touring center.

Here is a Revolutionary War farmstead in the gently rolling
landscape near Mt. Monadnock that has served as equestrian
land for nearly thirty years. Ezra Jackson was a homesteader
on this 600-acre tract in 1778. At first snowfall the bridle paths
are instantly transformed into cross-country trails that are
well conceived and cared for. The ski terrain varies from open
meadows to deep wooded forests and sudden clearings that
look out over the Green Mountains of southern Vermont: Monadnock, Ascutney, Stratton, Bromley, Haystack, Snow, and
Lake Spofford—a 40-mile vista. After the 30 kilometers are
exhausted—rather impossible even in a season of regular vis-
its—skiers can access the large forests of the 12,000-acre
Pisgah Wilderness Area, a region where ungroomed logging
trails and paths course endlessly. Rentals are available at
Road's End Farm, as well as informal instruction by appointment.

THE DARBY FIELD INN
Box D, Bald Inn
Conway, New Hampshire 03818
603-447-2181

Hours: Daylight.
Trail System: 18 kilometers (about 10 miles).
Trail Difficulty: Easiest, more difficult, most difficult.
Trail Grooming: Yes.
Rental Equipment: No.

Instruction: No.
Food Facilities: Dining room for breakfast and dinner.
Lodging: 17 rooms in the inn.
How to Get There: I-93 to Exit 24; Route 3 north to Route 25, northeast to Route 16; north to Bald Hill.

The top of Bald Hill is an eagle eye's panorama of the Mount Washington Valley and the whole Presidential Range. The scenery is as stunning as any you'll find in New England ski country, and the setting is an inn converted from a big farmhouse—now offering 17 bedrooms. From quaint Victorian interiors to the breadth of the New Hampshire mountain sky, the Darby Field Inn is a good choice for nearly any touring skier. After a day of tough running or just leisurely plodding through woods, the sunset view of the valley from the dining room is an amazing delight.

The trails themselves have a nice variety; they are only partially groomed and tracked, and draw skiers through hilly, wooded terrain. Skiers wanting more terrain can easily jump into the White Mountain National Forest, less than one kilometer from the take-off point at the inn. Equipment rentals, instruction, waxing advice, and the like are not available at the inn, but the ski town of North Conway is just a few miles away.

THE BALSAMS WILDERNESS
Dixville Notch, New Hampshire 03576
603-255-3400 or
800-255-0600 (continental U.S.) or
800-255-0800 (N.H.)

Hours: 9 a.m. to 4 p.m.
Trail System: 50 kilometers (31 miles).
Trail Difficulty: Easiest, more difficult, most difficult.
Trail Grooming: 40 kilometers double trackset by machine.
Rental Equipment: Cross-country and Telemark.
Instruction: Yes.
Food Facilities: Dining at the Balsams.
Lodging: More than 230 rooms in the Grand Balsams Resort Hotel.

How to Get There: I-93 to Lincoln, New Hampshire; Route 3 to Colebrook, and east on Route 26 to Dixville Notch. Alternate route from Boston: I-95 to Portsmouth; Route 16 to Route 26; west to Dixville Notch.

As a downhill area, the Balsams Wilderness "estate" has gained the reputation as one of the most pampering ski experiences in New England, and that holds for cross-country aficionados as well. Elsewhere, we have discussed the advantages of a cross-country area that can share the amenities and atmosphere of an established downhill area on the same premises—restaurants, lodges, housing, and the trail system, to name a few. For diners the gourmet experience at the Balsams is not one to be taken lightly, no matter what your ski preference. The Grand Balsams Resort Hotel has more than 230 rooms, and the management does not care if your skis are skinny, wide, or a little of each. Rental and retail gear is available for both Alpine and Nordic.

That said, the touring experience can certainly stand on its own merits here. The trail system is set in the fortress wall of the White Mountains entrance of Dixville Notch. There is wonderful scenic wilderness throughout the region, both on the well-groomed trackset trails, and the outback wilderness trails that meander across the estate.

MOOSE MOUNTAIN LODGE
Etna, New Hampshire 03750
603-643-3529

Hours: Dawn to dusk.
Trail System: 32 kilometers (about 50 miles).
Trail Difficulty: Easiest, more difficult, most difficult.
Trail Grooming: No.
Rental Equipment: Yes.
Instruction: Informal teaching is included with the lodge stay.
Food Facilities: For guests only, 3 meals daily.
Lodging: 12 guest rooms.

How to Get There: I-89 to Exit 18; Route 120 north for a half-mile to a right turn on Etna Road; turn right again one-half mile beyond the Etna Store onto Rudsboro Road; then 2 miles to a left turn onto Dana Road. Go one-half mile, then turn right up hill. Caution: At times this is tricky terrain to negotiate by car. Please call ahead.

Once an Alpine area in the formative days of the sport (1930s), Moose Mountain was converted into a ski-touring center that commands the lovely sweep of the Green Mountains and the Connecticut River Valley. Ghosts of those pioneer skiers seem still with the place, though now Kay and Peter Shumway operate the area solely as an inn, with ski touring a feature attraction for guests only. The area lacks public facilities, and at times the steep ascent up Moose Mountain is accessible only to overland vehicles. The area features a trail system that begins uphill at the front door of the inn. Skiers skim quickly into the fir woodlands, and then run down through exhilarating chutes out into dazzling open meadows. Here, the Appalachian Trail crosses, and skiers can use the many trails established by the Dartmouth Outing Club. The interior of the lodge encourages folks who have long since traded in the crowded nightlife for lingering home-cooked meals in front of radiant stone fireplaces.

TORY PINES
Route 47
Francestown, New Hampshire 03043
603-588-6352

Hours: 9 a.m. to 4:30 p.m.
Trail System: 50 kilometers (combined with Crotched Mountain trails).
Trail Difficulty: Easiest, more difficult, most difficult.
Trail Grooming: Daily.
Rental Equipment: 125 sets.
Instruction: Yes.
Food Facilities: Restaurant in the center of trail system.

Lodging: 35 rooms in the hotel.

How to Get There: Take I-91 to Brattleboro, Vermont; Route 9 east to Keene, New Hampshire; Route 101 east to Route 202; north on Route 202 to Route 47 and then east to Tory Pines.

For the first time last year, Tory Pines combined efforts with Crotched Mountain to operate a 50-kilometer groomed, track-set, marked, and patrolled trail system. This boosts the Tory Pine traditional system by about 20 kilometers, and opens the ski terrain into some hilly challenges and real cruising destinations for lunchtime stops. The areas combine their efforts also on the purchase of rental equipment, retail gear, and instruction—including Telemarking, which makes use of Crotched's downhill slopes. There is special attention here to beginners, who can purchase attractive lesson/rental/trail pass packages. Night skiing and Alpine are also available.

Tory itself is a 400-acre spread at the foot of Crotched, and offers skiing over open golf course terrain, dense woods that opens suddenly into spectacular views of the Monadnock region of lakes and mountains. All trails seem to lead eventually to a wonderful Revolutionary-period tavern that features fireside wine sipping and gourmet cuisine.

CANNON MOUNTAIN
Franconia, New Hampshire 03580
603-823-5563

Hours: 8 a.m. to 4:30 p.m.

Trail System: 8 kilometers (about 5 miles).

Trail Difficulty: Easiest, more difficult.

Trail Grooming: None.

Rental Equipment: Yes.

Instruction: By appointment.

Food Facilities: Restaurants nearby; a snack bar and cafeteria at the mountain.

Lodging: Motels and inns in the region.

How to Get There: I-93 to Lincoln, then Route 3 to Franconia Notch; Route 18 west to Echo Lake parking lot.

Cannon is one of the woolliest of the old-time ski areas. It was hewn out of the rugged granite uplands back in the skimeister days of the 1930s before disciplines were so specialized. Thus, it is possible that the Nansen Ski Club, first ski-touring organization in the nation, skinned their way up Cannon and jumped off the edge of the earth for a shot down the Taft Highway. These days, of course, there is a full, smallish, Nordic trail system as well as the Alpine area of Cannon. The Nordic area is rather casual, but pretty. Nordic skiers leave from the Echo Lake parking lot at Franconia Notch State Park, and run in the woodlands at the base of these granite towers. The trail system is within the state park, and instruction and rentals are available—by arrangement—at the Peabody Slopes Building.

FRANCONIA INN CROSS-COUNTRY SKI CENTER
Route 116, Easton Road
Franconia, New Hampshire 03580
603-823-5542

Hours: 9 a.m. to 5 p.m.
Trail System: 100 kilometers (about 62 miles).
Trail Difficulty: Easiest, more difficult, most difficult.
Trail Grooming: 64 kilometers groomed daily.
Rental Equipment: Yes.
Instruction: Yes.
Food Facilities: Restaurant at the inn.
Lodging: Rooms available at the inn.
How to Get There: I-93 to Lincoln, New Hampshire; Route 3 north to I-93 to Exit 38; Route 116 for 2 miles to the inn.

Located in one of the historic mountain settings of the Northeast, this ski area offers a view of the notch, of the Kinsman Range, of Mt. Lafayette, and the entire eastern valley of the White Mountain Range. It is land steeped in outdoor history. It is also quite demanding in spots, groomed with a lovely touch, and easily accessible from Boston. The trail system itself, spread out through the granite knobs and fir-forest-terrain of the region, is a healthy 65 miles, and ranges from gently sloped meadows to high shoulder skiing. With the number of motels, inns, and restaurants surrounding this trail system, it is fun to make a loop of many days. Maps are available showing you just how to do this.

Franconia Inn itself is a pleasant facility, and the barn beside it is a good retail shop for waxes and gear, instruction, contacts with guides, and box lunches for the trail. The inn is a fine destination for skiers who want to keep coming back.

GOFFSTOWN COUNTRY CLUB
The Donahues
Country Club Drive, Route 1
Goffstown, New Hampshire 03045
603-774-5031

Hours: 9 a.m. to 5 p.m.
Trail System: 22 kilometers (about 14 miles).
Trail Difficulty: Easiest, more difficult.
Trail Grooming: Yes.
Rental Equipment: Yes.
Instruction: Yes.
Food Facilities: Restaurant at the clubhouse.
Lodging: Several inns and motels within 4 miles of the center.
How to Get There: I-93 to Route 101; turn onto Route 114 in Goffstown and follow Route 13 North for 4 miles to the country club.

Goffstown Country Club is a fine example of good ski touring on golf course terrain and surrounding countryside. It is a day-tripper's area, encompassing open-field, trackset skiing with some off-the-trail powder-breaking as well. This area operates at a leisurely pace, and novices can benefit in a low-pressure environment from the good instruction and gentle terrain.

AMC PINKHAM NOTCH CAMP
Box 298
Gorham, New Hampshire 03581
603-466-2725

Hours: Daylight.
Trail System: 50 kilometers (31 miles).
Trail Difficulty: Easiest, more difficult, most difficult.
Trail Grooming: None.
Rental Equipment: None.
Instruction: No formal program.
Food Facilities: Breakfast and dinner at base camp. Trail lunches available if ordered the night before. Buffet lunches on weekends.
Lodging: Capacity for more than 100 persons; reservations advised. Dormitory-style bunking; shared baths.
How to Get There: I-95 to the Spaulding Turnpike to Route 16. Camp in 17 miles north of North Conway.

The AMC Camp at Pinkham Notch, the base of Mt. Washington, is one of the original outback mountaineering camps in New England. It is for the serious of purpose, the skillful, the experienced skier. That said, Pinkham Notch Camp also provides some of the greatest wilderness skiing anywhere. In places the trails are tied in with the Jackson Ski Touring facility, which is of a similar stripe. Along with individual skiing, there are several programs available, including weekend workshops, winter camping and snowshoeing, Telemarking, and photography. There are also evening programs and lectures.

Located at the eastern base of Mt. Washington in the heart of the White Mountain National Forest, the Pinkham Camp opens onto the rolling terrain of the shoulders of the Presidential Range, including the downhill area of Wildcat. This is some of the most breathtaking scenery in the Northeast, and there are several choices. One stimulating six-miler is the Avalanche Brook Ski Trail, connecting Pinkham Notch Camp with the Dana Place Inn to the south. This trail climbs nearly 1,000 feet, then drops 1,500 feet through fir and hardwood thicket.

You'll cross bridges over streams, then end with a one-mile run over Rocky Branch Trail and a meadow surrounding the Dana Place Inn.

This is one of the typical Pinkham Camp trails, and the most adventurous can pick up the trail from Jackson on this route. Described as "challenging skiing," what that really means is knowing what you're about. Don't attempt it alone or in bad skiing conditions. On the other hand, the reward of such a trail is some of the most exhilarating skiing in New England.

EASTMAN SKI TOURING CENTER
Box 53
Grantham, New Hampshire 03753
603-863-4500

Hours: 9 a.m. to 4 p.m.
Trail System: 30 kilometers (about 19 miles).
Trail Difficulty: Easiest, more difficult, most difficult.
Trail Grooming: Groomed and double trackset.
Rental Equipment: Yes.
Instruction: Group and semi-private lessons including Telemark.
Food Facilities: Harvey's Restaurant at the center serves drinks and lunch.
Lodging: Inns and motels in the area.
How to Get There: I-93 to I-89 north at Bow, New Hampshire, to Exit 13 at Grantham; turn right; the Eastman road is less than a half-mile on the right.

Eastman is a lovely four-season vacation resort spread out in the pine valley of the Sugar River in the west-central region of the state. The well-marked and cared for trail system encompasses all the features of the resort: golf course, woods, rolling hills including a small Alpine slope, and stream beds that feed into Eastman Pond. Novice skiers can work on the relative flats of Lazy Loop around the golf course, and as they get adventurous, work out into the woods loops. The 5-kilometer

Deerpath Loop will test anyone's skills, and for distance, skirting Eastman Pond can be close to a 10-kilometer project. The countryside is pretty, with views of the surrounding mountains, and the amenities at the center are complete: rental and retail shop, waxing area, and ready instruction. At the center, Harvey's is a good-sized lounge that serves drinks and a limited lunch menu.

THE LEDGES FARM
Grantham, New Hampshire 03753
603-863-1002

Hours: 7 a.m. to 4 p.m.
Trail System: 80 kilometers (about 66 miles).
Trail Difficulty: Easiest, more difficult, most difficult.
Trail Grooming: 30 miles of trails are regularly groomed and trackset.
Rental Equipment: Yes.
Instruction: Yes.
Food Facilities: Yes.
Lodging: At the Ledges.
How to Get There: I-93 to I-89, follow to Exit 13; turn south for one-quarter mile.

In the heart of the Lake Sunapee-Dartmouth-Eastman region of the state, the Ledges (formerly Grey Ledges) is a farm dating to the Revolutionary War period. It is mostly open pastureland that runs down to the broad valley of the Sugar River, along old stone walls and up into the hardwood thickets that once separated farms in the area. Several old logging roads lead out of the meadows and into the high country, from which skiers overlook the many ponds and lakes of the Sunapee region. Horseback riding, snowshoeing, and moonlight excursions are all part of the tourer's experience at The Ledges. Between the main lodge, motel, bunk houses, and family rooms, the center can handle individual skiers, or gangs as large as one hundred people. The home cooking in the Hob Grille is excellent, and there is entertainment on the weekends. The area is in the heart of ski country—40 minutes to Woodstock, Vermont, 1½ hours to Stowe. As a touring center The Ledges Farm stands up superbly to these areas around it.

HOLLIS HOF SKI TOURING CENTER

53 Richardson Road
Hollis, New Hampshire 03049
603-465-2633

Hours: 9 a.m. to 5 p.m.
Trail System: 18 kilometers (about 10 miles).
Trail Difficulty: Easiest.
Trail Grooming: Groomed and trackset.
Rental Equipment: Yes.
Instruction: Yes.
Food Facilities: Snack bar on premises; restaurant is 1 mile distant.
Lodging: Motels available in Nashua, 7 miles distant.
How to Get There: Route 128 to Route 3; then Route 130 west to Hollis; then Depot Road to Richardson Road and the Touring Center.

Hollis Hof is a good day trip for the Boston-area skier who wants an injection of New Hampshire countryside for little effort or drive. The area is just seven miles out of Nashua, New Hampshire. It provides gentle field and surrounding woods skiing on ungroomed conditions, though tracks are always set by skiers who went before. The area has 100 sets of skis to rent, and makes instruction available on request. Hollis Hof is mainly a weekend area, though it will open during the week by appointment. Ask for Charles Beebe, who runs the area with his wife, Lucie.

INTERVALE NORDIC LEARNING CENTER
Route 16A
Intervale, New Hampshire 03845
603-356-3379

Hours: 9 a.m. to 5 p.m., December 15 to March 1.
Trail System: 35 kilometers of groomed trail with 50 kilometers overall (about 31 miles).
Trail Difficulty: Easiest, more difficult, most difficult.
Trail Grooming: Trackset over 35 kilometers.
Rental Equipment: Yes.
Instruction: PSIA-certified ski school.
Food Facilities: Several nearby restaurants.
Lodging: Two country inns, two motor lodges, and one bed and breakfast facility within 200 yards of the center.
How to Get There: I-93 to Exit 24; Route 3 north to Route 25; northeast to Route 16, north through Conway and North Conway; then Route 16A 3 miles to the learning center.

Located in the Mount Washington Valley, the Intervale Learning Center is dedicated to the proposition that skiers at any level can learn a thing or twenty about the sport. The instructors are as fun as they are effective, and will eventually want to work you out on the hillside. The trails are well marked and groomed, most of them offering nice views of Mt. Washington and the Moat Range. Skiers will use many of the old logging roads that criss-cross the region, and some may opt to climb the saddle of Bartlett Mountain with its scenic overlooks. These contain woodstove-heated warming huts along the way. In addition, there is the annual Christmas Eve tree-lighting ceremony, and several moonlight and cookout tours through the season.

JACKSON SKI TOURING FOUNDATION
Jackson, New Hampshire 03846
603-383-9355

Hours: 8:30 a.m. to 5 p.m.
Trail System: 140 kilometers (about 88 miles).
Trail Difficulty: Easiest, more difficult, most difficult.
Trail Grooming: 60 kilometers groomed daily.
Rental Equipment: Yes.
Instruction: PSIA-certified.
Food Facilities: Several nearby restaurants.
Lodging: Several inns and motels in the area.
How to Get There: I-93 to Exit 24; Route 3 north to Route 25, northeast to Route 16; then north through North Conway into Jackson.

Aside from its legendary stature as the historic capital of cross-country skiing, and with plenty of echoes of the skimeister days when it took all morning to "skin" up Black Mountain for one run down, the village of Jackson is simply astoundingly beautiful. Classic New England is what you get here, from the old covered bridge that welcomes you into town to the white church in the center of the village, and the exciting pace of serious ski touring—all under the command of Mt. Washington.

Do not be deterred by the talk of serious skiing, however. True, from start to finish Jackson exudes the sport. But still, there's plenty here for the novice, the snowshoer, hiker, the vacationer simply looking for delicious mountain experience.

Jackson truly goes to the roots of the region. It is a nonprofit operation that combines the efforts of the U.S. Forest Service and several private landowners. Since the 1970s it has been incorporated for the sole purpose of advancing crosscountry skiing. Of the 140 kilometers of trails, 60 are groomed carefully, and often. Skiers wind through hardwood forestland, open-gladed meadows, and upland wilderness that leads into the shoulders of the Presidential Range. Across the river and into the trees, the Ellis River Trail winds in a long, slightly uphill loop along the river to a woodland inn; the way home is an easy downhill breezer all the way back to the road. For offtrack skiers there is ample opportunity for backpacking and camping trips into the backlands on mountain skis.

At the Jackson Ski Touring Foundation building you will find the Jack Frost Ski Shop that will rent or sell equipment, and all kinds of retail accessories. Here you can sign up for a lesson, take a waxing clinic, or sign up for a night-skiing foray. And, finally, for the inexhaustible, Jackson and its environs has a full lineup of terrific nightlife.

WOODBOUND INN
Jaffrey, New Hampshire 03452
603-532-8341

Hours: 9 a.m. to 5:30 p.m.
Trail System: 32 kilometers (about 20 miles).
Trail Difficulty: Easiest, more difficult, most difficult.

Trail Grooming: As needed.
Rental Equipment: 120 sets.
Instruction: Yes.
Food Facilities: Restaurant at the inn.
Lodging: Rooms at the inn.
How to Get There: Route 2 in Massachusetts to Route 202, then
    north into New Hampshire and to Woodbound.

With 32 kilometers of nicely set tracks opening into the state forest land—not to mention two downhill practice slopes for Telemark work—Woodbound has a total ski experience to offer its guests. The trail system varies from gently rolling flattish land, with running tracks, to wilderness shots up, down, and all around through the public lands.

In addition, Woodbound offers the extras for everyone to enjoy all the little corners of winter—from night tobogganing down specially sculpted chutes, to ice skating and sleigh rides, then indoors for movies, square dances, and cider parties. The food is homemade and renowned in ski country.

GUNSTOCK SKI TOURING CENTER
Box 336
Laconia, New Hampshire 03246
603-293-4341

Hours: 8:30 a.m. to 4:30 p.m.
Trail System: 25 kilometers (about 16 miles).
Trail Difficulty: Easiest, more difficult, most difficult.
Trail Grooming: As needed, double trackset.
Rental Equipment: 100 sets.
Instruction: All ability levels, including Telemark.
Food Facilities: Cafeteria in the main ski lodge.
Lodging: Several motels and inns nearby.
How to Get There: I-93 to Exit 20; Route 3 to Route 11A; follow
    to Gunstock.

With its 15-kilometer zinger, where several U.S. Nordic Combined championships have been held, to its gentle trails that wind the novice skier through some lovely winter woods, Gunstock offers the entire spectrum of the sport. And as with many Alpine-Nordic combinations, cross-country skiing here shares the amenities of the well-established downhill facility. Yet, there is a rustic Touring Center that seems built around a huge woodstove, and offers Nordic aficionados everything they will want or need. The intermediate trails are pretty and varied. Skiing begins on farm fields sectioned by ancient stone walls, then to brookside trails that run through cathedral-like stands of pine and birch forest. There is plenty of touring off the trail as well, leading experts up the flank of Mt. Cobble and into the notch between Cobble and Gunstock. From the high terrain you overlook Lake Winnipesaukee. From here, for the hearty, there is a 3-mile racing loop that skirts Cobble and returns to the hospitable baselodge.

LOON MOUNTAIN SKI TOURING
Route 112, Loon Mountain Road
Lincoln, New Hampshire 03251
603-745-8111, Extension 568

Hours: 8:30 a.m. to 4:30 p.m.
Trail System: 30 kilometers (about 19 miles).
Trail Difficulty: Easiest, more difficult, most difficult.
Trail Grooming: As needed.
Rental Equipment: Yes.
Instruction: Yes.
Food Facilities: Lunches available at the base lodge.
Lodging: A 40-unit inn at the mountain, as well as several rental condominiums through the Loon reservation service.
How to Get There: I-93 to Exit 32; Route 112 east in New Hampshire, then Loon Mountain Road.

Though touring at this popular Alpine area has all the advantages and drawbacks that go along with sharing facilities with downhill types, the Loon trails lead you quickly into the wilderness of the Pemigewasset National Forest. Skiing here follows a spider web of old logging roads and deer paths, with sudden views of the Franconia Range of the White Mountains. Trails course through the deep solitude of snow-impacted stream beds, and slab up the sides of steep hills in spots. They are well marked. The trail system also employs the Alpine slopes for you to go out on your Telemark skinny skis and show the jellybeans what real skiing is. The nightlife at Loon holds countless opportunities for the tireless.

LOCH LYME LODGE
Lyme, New Hampshire 03768
603-795-2141

Hours: Dawn to dusk, beginning the day after Christmas.
Trail System: Roughly 16 kilometers (10 miles).
Trail Difficulty: Easiest, more difficult.
Trail Grooming: None.
Rental Equipment: No.
Instruction: No.
Food Facilities: Breakfast at the lodge.
Lodging: Rooms at the lodge.
How to Get There: I-91 to Exit 14 at Thetford, Vermont; then
    Route 10 north to Loch Lyme.

This area centers around the experience of a Revolutionary-period farmhouse converted to an inn that dates back to 1924. Though the summer capacity of the area is expanded by 25 cabins on the property, the winter limit is around 10. In winter, the inn is run as a bed and breakfast establishment with cross-country skiing available for guests. The area is not open for day skiers who are not guests.

The small winter contingent at the inn often melds into a convivial little core of skiers and lodgers who share their experiences of skiing on this lovely forested 100 acres. Unplowed paths course through the forest; some routes take in the lake, lakeshore, and fields of the area. Moonlight tours are also available. This is a perfect area for the skier with some experience who has his own equipment, though the nearby town of Lyme, with some prior arrangement, has rentals and retail gear available.

WINDBLOWN
New Ipswich, New Hampshire 03071
603-878-2869

Hours: 9 a.m. to 5 p.m.
Trail System: 30 kilometers (about 19 miles).
Trail Difficulty: Easiest, more difficult, most difficult.
Trail Grooming: 15 kilometers groomed daily.
Rental Equipment: 100 sets.
Instruction: Weekends; by appointment on weekdays.
Food Facilities: Meals served at The Kitchen on weekends, holidays, and vacations. Soup and sandwich available during week.
Lodging: Inns and motels in the area.
How to Get There: I-495 to Route 119 northwest to West Townsend, Massachusetts; Route 124 through New Ipswich, then Route 124 into New Hampshire and Windblown.

This high-elevation touring center in the sweeping Monadnock countryside usually has a long season, pushing well into April most years. It is a full-amenity center with a good baselodge complete with rentals, retail shop, waxing room, and a simple hearty kitchen for trail's end when skiers kick their feet up in front of the radiant woodstove. Deep in the middle of the 20-mile trail system there is a warming hut in the woods for ski-hikers to lay out a bedroll for the night, or for day skiers to stop for lunch.

NORSK SKI TOURING CENTER

Route 11
New London, New Hampshire 03257
603-526-4685

Hours: 9 a.m. to 5 p.m.
Trail System: 50 kilometers (about 31 miles).
Trail Difficulty: Easiest, more difficult, most difficult.
Trail Grooming: Groomed and trackset.
Rental Equipment: 100 sets.
Instruction: Classes at 10:30 a.m., noon, and 1 p.m.
Food Facilities: Restaurant and lounge on premises.
Lodging: Inn on the premises. Separate phone: 603-526-6040.
How to Get There: I-93 to I-89 to Exit 11; east 1½ miles past
    Grey House Restaurant to the first right-hand turn.

This touring center on the skirts Mt. Kearsarge offers some excellent large and varied terrain for touring in the region. All trails are well groomed and well marked; the loops are intelligently conceived for novice skiers looking for their first short loop, to the expert who wants to run a marathon through these foothills. One of the nicest features is that Norsk is a major-sized area just two hours from Boston near Sunapee and King Ridge—two Alpine areas made for Nordic whizzes who are ready to try out their Telemark technique. Norsk has a full spate of services, including rentals, retail gear, food, and lodging at the nice, white-gabled Lake Sunapee Country Club and Inn. Excellent maps are available, and special events— from moonlight tours to sauna tours to waxing workshops— are available to tourers.

CARROLL REED TOURING CENTER

Main Street
North Conway, New Hampshire 03860
603-356-3122 or 603-356-3200

Hours: 9 a.m. to 5 p.m.
Trail System: 25 kilometers (about 16 miles).
Trail Difficulty: Easiest, more difficult.

Trail Grooming: Daily.

Rental Equipment: 100 sets at center.

Instruction: By appointment.

Food Facilities: Restaurants in North Conway.

Lodging: Inns and motels in North Conway.

How to Get There: I-95 to Portsmouth, New Hampshire; Spaulding Turnpike to Route 16 through Conway to North Conway.

North Conway is in the original heart of ski country—Mount Washington Valley in the Presidential Range. It is a town of preppy chic overlooked by the stately Mt. Washington itself. The Carroll Reed shop in the center of town operates this touring center with 25 kilometers of nicely groomed trails that roll gently along the boulder-studded river roads with nice views of Washington and other Presidentials. Of course, skiers begin and end at this fashionable shop, a feature not overlooked by some Nordic fans. Also, along the golf course, part of the ski terrain, a new country club has been built; in the winter it serves skiers.

SAGAMORE-HAMPTON SKI TOURING CENTER

101 North Road

North Hampton, New Hampshire 03862

603-964-5341

Hours: 9 a.m. to 4 p.m.

Trail System: 30 kilometers (about 18 miles).

Trail Difficulty: Easiest, more difficult.

Trail Grooming: About 40 percent groomed and trackset.

Rental Equipment: 70 pairs.

Instruction: No.

Food Facilities: Snacks and refreshments available in clubhouse.

Lodging: Inns and motels in the area with bed and breakfast within 1 mile.

How to Get There: I-95 to Route 51; east on Route 101D, then north on Route 151 for 1 mile to the touring center.

Sagamore-Hampton is a large wooded wildlife sanctuary adjacent to an 18-hole golf course, where the touring center is located. About one-third of the ski terrain is over the open fields of the golf course, with the rest of it running through flat to gently rolling woods. This is not skiing to challenge experts, but is an excellent spot to learn and practice skiing. The center reserves the right to close in icy or treacherous conditions that arise in this coastal area. If there's a question, call ahead.

MOUNT CUBE SKI TOURING CENTER
Mount Cube Farm
Orford, New Hampshire 03777
603-353-4709

Hours: 8 a.m. to 5 p.m.
Trail System: 20 kilometers (about 13 miles) of groomed and marked trails.
Trail Difficulty: Easiest, more difficult, most difficult.
Trail Grooming: Yes.
Rental Equipment: Yes.
Instruction: By appointment.
Food Facilities: Breakfast, light trail lunches.
Lodging: Lyme Inn and Hobson House within 8 miles.
How to Get There: I-93 to Plymouth, New Hampshire, at Exit 27; Route 25 west for 8 miles to the center.

Mount Cube offers skiing over far-flung farm pastureland of Orford, New Hampshire, at the foot of the White Mountains. Its trail network traverses a variety of terrain, with several trails designed to provide views of spectacular White Mountains scenery. The Sugar House Lodge will get you started with a big breakfast of pancakes oozing with maple syrup produced at the farm. A full line of rentals and retail equipment is available.

DEER CAP SKI TOURING CENTER
Route 16
Ossipee, New Hampshire 03814
603-539-6030

Hours: 8:30 a.m. to 4:30 p.m.
Trail System: 20 kilometers (about 13 miles).
Trail Difficulty: Easiest, more difficult, most difficult.
Trail Grooming: Groomed and trackset as needed.
Rental Equipment: 100 sets.
Instruction: By appointment only.
Food Facilities: Trails snacks at the center.
Lodging: Inns and motels in the area within 2 miles.
How to Get There: I-95 to Portsmouth, New Hampshire; Spaulding Turnpike to Route 16 north to Center Ossipee.

Think you're a hotshot? Think you can bring a little place like Deer Cap to its knees with your dazzle? Then the Superstar trail is for you. Deer Cap may not have much expert terrain, but this windy, snaggy heart-stopper will be taken seriously by skiers on every level since it is one of the toughest you can find. Most of the trails here wind through pretty, fairly flat terrain in pine woods. The lodge has an eating center with a snack bar, rest rooms, and plenty of room to wax your skis. The trails begin just outside the door. In January this family-operated center sponsors a Cystic Fibrosis Tourathon.

PLAUSAWA VALLEY TOURING CENTER
Whitemore Road
Pembroke, New Hampshire 03301
603-224-6267

Hours: Weekends, holidays, and school vacations only, 9 a.m. to dusk.
Trail System: 12 kilometers (about 7 miles).
Trail Difficulty: Easiest, more difficult.
Trail Grooming: Groomed and trackset as needed.
Rental Equipment: Yes.

Instruction: No.
Food Facilities: Soups, light snacks at the center; full restaurants within 2 miles.
Lodging: Inns and motels in the area.
How to Get There: I-93 to Exit 13 south; Route 3 south for 2½ miles.

The Plausawa Valley Country Club offers some open-meadow skiing, though most of the trails are over wooded terrain that leads down along the Suncook River; one of the trails curls out far enough for an overlook of the Merrimack. Though most of the terrain is gentle stuff, watch out for one or two heart-pounding ascents—and of course descents—along the system. These are well marked, of course. Adjacent to the clubhouse is a lighted skating rink for the indefatigable; a few citizens races are held here as well. Call ahead, as Plausawa is not always open.

SARGEANT SKI TOURING CENTER
Boston University Human Environment Institute
RFD 2
Peterborough, New Hampshire 03458
603-525-3311 or 603-525-9342 (weekends).

Hours: Saturday and Sunday, 9 a.m. to 4 p.m.
Trail System: 32 kilometers (20 miles); designated snowshoe trails.
Trail Difficulty: Easiest, more difficult, most difficult.
Trail Grooming: As needed.
Rental Equipment: Ski-touring sets and snowshoes.
Instruction: Beginner and intermediate lessons; guided environmental ski tours.
Food Facilities: Snacks, soup, and soft drinks at the ski lodge.
Lodging: Write for reservation information.
How to Get There: I-91 to Brattleboro, Vermont, then Route 9 east to Keene, New Hampshire; Route 101 east to Peterborough, then Union Street west to Windy Row to the touring center.

Not a spot for day-ski touring, the Sargeant center is rather a four-seasons camp run by Boston University's Human Environment Institute, and dedicated to the pursuit of serious outdoor play in the splendid Mt. Monadnock region of the state. Generally catering to groups and club-type organizations, the Sargeant Camp offers weekend retreats, and a host of activities around the ski touring. There are outdoor skills workshops, hiking, and showshoeing in the winter, as well as adventure activities in the Outward Bound mold. This is all optional, of course.

The skiing terrain is spider-webbed with marked and groomed trails that take you out on 850 rolling acres of the Monadnock hills region. Terrain ranges from gentle pastureland to deep choppy woods skiing. There are plenty of experienced skiers at the center to help you on an informal basis; full lessons are available as well. Guests of the center stay in heated cabins with hot and cold water and showers, though you should bring your own bedding and toilet articles. Around the crackling fire in the dining room, guests are served three home-style meals daily. Caution: Reservations should be made well in advance; the center books up fast with the first scent of winter on the air. BU students and alumni get a 10-percent discount on lodging.

TEMPLE MOUNTAIN SKI CORPORATION
Route 101, Box 368
Peterborough, New Hampshire 03458
603-924-6949

Hours: Tuesday through Sunday, 9 a.m. to 4:30 p.m.
Trail System: 56 kilometers (about 35 miles).
Trail Difficulty: Easiest, more difficult, most difficult.
Trail Grooming: 8 kilometers groomed, 6 of them trackset.
Rental Equipment: More than 100 sets.
Instruction: Regular schedule, 9:45, noon, and 12:15. Also special Telemark clinics Wednesday nights at 7.
Food Facilities: Cafeteria and lounge in the main lodge.
Lodging: None on the mountain; several hotels, motels, and inns in the region.

How to Get There: Route 3 north to Nashua; Route 101A to 101
west to Peterborough to Temple Mountain.

Several improvements have changed this already excellent and
well-appointed ski-touring area. Many of the trails have been
widened and improved, with new terrain being opened all the
time. More and more of the terrain is being tracked than in
past years, and a new Telemark program has been designed,
making use of the broad downhill trails on Temple.

At an elevation between 1,500 and 2,000 feet, Temple usually records an annual snowfall of between ten and fourteen
feet, and is a paradise for powderhounds no matter what they
have on their feet. Add to this much snow the fact that Temple
is less than 70 miles from Boston, and you have the makings of
a major ski-touring area for the snow-starved folks from New
England's flatlands.

The skiing, which combines its own large system with the
20-mile Wapack Trail, takes tourers across fir-ringed mountain
ridges with sudden dramatic overlooks; then the trail may
plunge down across meadowland into hardwood groves and
stream beds. For the adventurous, narrower trails wind off
the beaten path through thickets of snow-heavy evergreen
boughs, and lead skiers into day-long wilderness tours. There
are several shelters scattered throughout the trail system. The
area also provides a full variety of skier services. Under new
management, Temple plans to add gourmet cuisine.

SNOWVILLAGE INN
Snowville, New Hampshire 03849
603-447-2818

Hours: 9 a.m. to dusk.
Trail System: 13 kilometers; downhill ski trails also available
    nearby.
Trail Difficulty: Easiest, more difficult.
Trail Grooming: Yes.
Rental Equipment: Yes.
Instruction: Weekends, or weekdays by appointment.

Food Facilities: Full meals and bar available at Snowvillage
   Inn.
Lodging: Snowvillage Inn, plus inns and motels throughout
   the Mount Washington Valley. Child care by reservation.
How to Get There: I-95 to Spaulding Turnpike to Route 16
   north to Conway; south on Route 153 to sign for Snowville
   and Brownfield; at Snowville, right on Foss Mountain
   Road.

With good reason, the Snowvillage Inn, an Edwardian estate
in the lap of Mt. Washington, 1,100 feet high in its foothills,
has gained the reputation as one of the most spectacular winter vacation spots in the region. Innkeepers Ginger and Pat-
rick Blymyer describe it as "a little out of way, a little out of
the ordinary." Both things are true. Though only 6 miles out of
Conway, the inn is secluded in the upper woodlands of Foss
Mountain; from the porch guests have a sweeping panoramic
view of the valley, with Mt. Washington itself looming over the
place, close enough to touch, it seems.

The skiing is of the woodland variety with groomed and
double-trackset trails (150 acres) that take skiers into thickets
and out again for sudden high-altitude overviews of the valley.
The skiing is lovely, convenient, and thoroughly accommo-
dated to tourers. But it is the inn that cuts Snowville above
the ordinary. With its 14 cozy bedrooms, the crackling fire in a
big country living room cluttered with books, magazines, and
dozing dogs, this inn is as honestly homey and convivial as
they come. In the oil-lamplight of the dining room guest are
served multi-course gourmet meals, beginning with perhaps
Hungarian mushroom soup and ending with cognac back at
the fire. It is difficult to exaggerate the elegance and charm of
the Snowvillage Inn in its après-ski mode.

Incidentally, the reference here is to the Blymyers' dogs;
guests' pets are not allowed, nor do any of the inn's dogs run
the ski trails.

SUNSET HILL HOUSE
Sugar Hill, New Hampshire 03585
603-823-5522

Hours: 8 a.m. to dusk.
Trail System: 40 kilometers (about 25 miles).
Trail Difficulty: Easiest, more difficult, most difficult.
Trail Grooming: 30 kilometers groomed daily.
Rental Equipment: Yes.
Instruction: Yes.
Food Facilities: Soup is served at the touring center; full meals at the inn.
Lodging: 35 rooms at the inn.
How to Get There: I-93 to Lincoln, New Hampshire; Route 3 north to I-93 again; then Route 117 west to Sunset Hill House.

Atop Sugar Hill in the White Mountains sits the Sunset House, an old New England inn with a nice flavor of its own, and excellent, nearly limitless skiing possibilites. Its own trails run into the Franconia Inn network, as well as a few other trail systems in this well-toured region. Skiers can slide all day over the lower flats of the valley, or chug up through the timber-ringed upper plateaus for an overview of the impressive geography of the region. Back at the Sunset Hill House, skiers like to hang out at the ski shop with its kettle of homemade soup simmering on the stove. All the amenities are available, from instruction to rental and retail equipment. This is also the place to sign up for guided day and moonlight tours. The inn has a fine restaurant for food and drink; it offers quality lodging.

THE INN AT EAST HILL FARM
Troy, New Hampshire 03465
603-242-6495

Hours: Daylight.
Trail System: 20 kilometers (about 13 miles).
Trail Difficulty: Easiest, more difficult, most difficult.
Trail Grooming: As needed.
Rental Equipment: Yes.
Instruction: Yes.
Food Facilities: Full restaurant at the inn.
Lodging: Cottages available; rooms at the inn.
How to Get There: I-91 to Brattleboro, Vermont; Route 9 east to Keene, New Hampshire; Route 12 south to Troy; left on Jaffrey Road to the inn.

East Hill Farm is one of those country inns that, while not monumental in size and scope, do many things with excellence. Most notably, the trail system, sledding, tobogganing, hiking on the rolling countryside—all the terrain here is gentle and appealing, with its lovely scenery around the base of Mt. Monadnock. The farm itself is also appealing, producing delicious country-style meals and offering square dances, indoor swimming, sauna, and a skating rink. East Hill Farm is a complete and well-appointed touring destination.

WATERVILLE VALLEY SKI TOURING CENTER
Waterville Valley, New Hampshire 03223
603-236-8351

Hours: 9 a.m. to 4:30 p.m.
Trail System: 60 kilometers (about 38 miles).
Trail Difficulty: Easiest, more difficult, most difficult.
Trail Grooming: Yes.
Rental Equipment: Yes.
Instruction: PSIA-certified.
Food Facilities: Finish Line Restaurant at the Touring Center.
Lodging: Several inns, rental condominiums, and motels in
    the area.
How to Get There: I-93 north to Exit 28; Route 49 north to
    Waterville Valley.

Waterville Valley is one of the major Alpine ski centers in the
Northeast, and in recent years has become a self-contained ski
village for all sizes, styles, and levels of the sport. Using all the
meadows and woods in the region, cross-country buffs have
nearly unlimited touring. On the more organized trail system,
skiers will follow miles of old logging roads, starting from a
cluster of rustic buildings that comprise the center. The trail
web rolls outward from this spot, a carefully graded, marked,
and groomed system. Some trails roll through gentle woodland flats, while others mount precipitously toward high-country plateaus and nice vistas of the surrounding mountains.
Alpine and Nordic forms mix at Waterville when it is time for
coaches at the school to give Telemark instruction. The teaching also features demonstrations, workshops of all kinds, and
video-teaching. For beginners, there is a fine special "starter
kit" to get you rolling with a day of free rentals and no trail
fee. Look for a full complement of rental and retail goods, and
ask about the race program. This is a World Class ski area
with many top-shelf events in its list of credits. For those who
like nightlife and/or elegant dining, there are some good bars
and restaurants in the village.

THE NORDIC SKIER
19 North Main Street
Wolfeboro, New Hampshire 03894
603-569-3151

Hours: 9 a.m. to 5:30 p.m.
Trail System: 20 kilometers (about 13 miles).
Trail Difficulty: Easiest, more difficult.
Trail Grooming: Yes.
Rental Equipment: Yes.
Instruction: PSIA-certified.
Food Facilities: In the town and area.
Lodging: In the town and area.
How to Get There: I-93 to Hooksett; Route 28 to Wolfeboro. Or
    I-95 to the Spaulding Turnpike to Lake Winnipesaukee;
    then Route 11 north to Wolfeboro.

Wolfeboro is a fishing town. Summer and winter, the folks talk
fishing, anticipate it, clean up after it, and get ready for more.
Yet there is a certain season after the first snow falls in No-
vember, when another kind of sportsman comes into Wolfeboro—the touring skier. Along with snowmobilers and ice
fishermen, the town also becomes the cross-country center of
the Lakes Region. There are two separate trail systems that
offer a variety of experiences (though without the real toe-
curling black terrain)—the more challenging Abenaki Trails,
and the Lakeview network for novice or easy skiing. There are
also plenty of woods, unplowed logging roads, and wilderness
skiing for off-track aficionados. There is a good touring spe-
cialty shop at hand in Wolfeboro as the town has come to cater
to skiers. Rentals, guides, retail gear, instruction, and all sorts
of moonlight skiing and workshops are available here as well.
Good food and lodging abound in wide variety.

MAINE

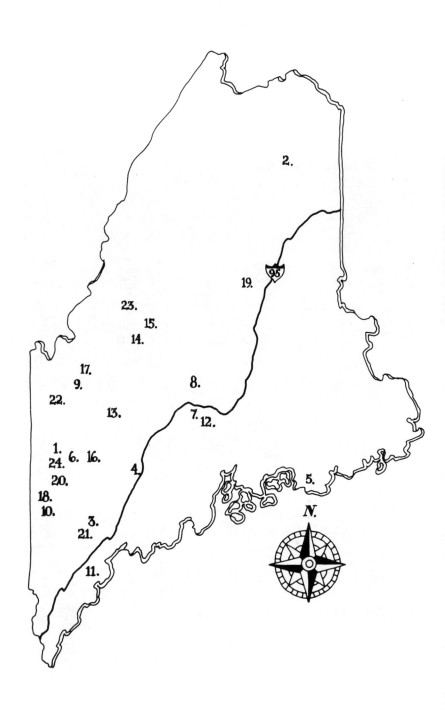

2.

19. 95

23.

15.

14.

17.

9.

8.

22.

13.

7. 12.

1.

24. 6. 16.

4.

20.

5.

N.

18.

10.

3.

21.

11.

Maine

Numbers on map refer to towns numbered below

AKERS SKI TOURING CENTER
Andover, Maine 04216
207-392-4582

Hours: Dawn to dusk.
Trail System: 10 kilometers (about 6 miles).
Trail Difficulty: Easiest, more difficult, most difficult.
Trail Grooming: Yes.
Rental Equipment: Yes.
Instruction: No.
Food Facilities: At the center.
Lodging: Within 20 minutes of the center, at Rumford or Bethel, Maine.
How to Get There: Maine Turnpike and I-95 to Fairfield, Maine, then Route 201 north to Skowhegan; Route 2 through Rumford to Route 5 north to Andover.

The Akers is a serious ski facility that draws the entire spectrum—from picnicking families to the runners in racing suits. Interlacing loops of trails are designed for the various uses, and signs state clearly whether a loop is for racers only (black course) or open touring (blue course). The touring trails wind upward more than 300 feet, and give skiers a nice overlook of the tidy New England village of Andover, along with the Telstar earth satellite station below. Skiers heading west from the back door of the center can warm up on flats, then plunge into the forested Spring Water Loop that stops at the overlook, then meander far out to the Sap Run before returning through the forest again. These trails have a variety of difficulty, so follow signs. When the trail map says "steep," the Akers are talking steep. The main touring of the area, however, is gentle, pretty, and worth the drive. A very well-stocked Nordic store is available at the center.

AROOSTOCK SKI TOURING CENTER
Wrightville Road, Box 291
Ashland, Maine 04732
207-435-6076

Hours: Dawn to dusk.
Trail System: 10 kilometers (about 6 miles).
Trail Difficulty: Easiest, more difficult, most difficult.
Trail Grooming: Groomed and trackset.
Rental Equipment: Yes.
Instruction: Yes.
Food Facilities: Coffee and doughnuts at the center; restaurant
    in nearby Ashland.
Lodging: Motels available in Ashland.
How to Get There: I-95 north to Route 212 to Route 11; follow
    to Wrightville Road to the touring center.

This northern Maine center combines the flats and gently rolling hills of "potato country" with fine woodland wilderness
skiing. Most of the skiing, in fact, is in a woods setting, with
some nice open meadows. Some of the trail loops are steep
and windy, offering plenty of challenge to the advanced skier.
Aroostock County logging roads make for fine wilderness touring as well.

SNORADA RECREATION CENTER
525 Lake Street
Auburn, Maine 04210
207-782-6602

Hours: Monday through Friday, 11 a.m. to 9 p.m.; weekends, 9
    a.m. to 9 p.m. (Night skiing on a lighted trail loop.)
Trail System: 15 kilometers (about 10 miles).
Trail Difficulty: Easiest, more difficult, most difficult.
Trail Grooming: Groomed and trackset.
Rental Equipment: Yes.
Instruction: Lessons by appointment.
Food Facilities: Snack bar at center; full restaurants within
    one-half mile of the center.

Lodging: In Auburn.

How to Get There: Maine Turnpike to Exit 12 in Auburn; after
    tolls take a left on Washington Avenue and follow down-
    town through three sets of lights. Left on Court Street and
    bear right onto Lake Street; the center is about 2 miles up
    Lake Street.

This cosmopolitan touring center is the site of the Bates College Winter Carnival, and plenty of citizen racing, including a
Bill Koch League and Tuesday night races that give it a rather
vigorous cast. The terrain varies from open field to some
woods running loops, over two somewhat challenging ridges
and across a frozen lake. It is fine touring, and there are plans
to expand the trail system. The center has rental and retail
equipment, and provides a waxing room and trail snacks.

NATANIS CROSS-COUNTRY SKI TRAILS
RFD 1, Box 554
Augusta, Maine 04330
27-622-6533

Hours: Weekdays, 9 a.m. to 4 p.m.; weekends, 8 a.m. to 4 p.m.

Trail System: 10 kilometers (about 6 miles).

Trail Difficulty: Easiest, more difficult.

Trail Grooming: Trackset.

Rental Equipment: Yes.

Instruction: For beginners.

Food Facilities: Trail snacks available at the center; full restau-
    rant meals within 4 miles.

Lodging: Motel within 4 miles.

How to Get There: Maine Turnpike to Augusta, then Route 201
    north. After passing Cony High School in Augusta, the
    center is 8 miles on Route 201.

Beginning with open field warm-ups, the Natanis trails take
skiers through deep forest trails where, despite the proximity
to the city, an abundance of wildlife makes its presence
known. You'll see signs of moose, deer, rabbit, and fox as you

ski over this rolling terrain. One trail leads out to a beaver bog, where the animals have felled trees to build their lodges to hibernate the winter away. Not a heavy challenge for the mountain-man skier, Natanis is nevertheless a pretty, well-run ski area. Town-sponsored citizen races and moonlight tours are part of the fun here.

ACADIA NATIONAL PARK
Box 177
Bar Harbor, Maine 04609
207-288-3338

Hours: 24 hours a day; headquarters, 8:30 a.m. to 4:30 p.m.
Trail System: 79 kilometers (about 49 miles) for ski touring and snowshoeing only.
Trail Difficulty: Easiest, more difficult.
Trail Grooming: None.
Rental Equipment: Ski shops in the area.
Instruction: None.
Food Facilities: Nearby.
Lodging: Nearby.
How to Get There: Maine Turnpike to Route 3, follow through Ellsworth to Bar Harbor; right on Route 233 for 3 miles to park headquarters.

Acadia National Park is one of the splendid natural wonders of New England and a long-standing attraction for millions of summertime visitors. In winter, however, this coastal forest with its glimpses of the stormy, rock-bound coast and the steady sea-roar is quite a moving experience for most skiers. Nature can overwhelm you here just a bit, and you return, even from a three-hour trip, feeling you have been far away for a long time. The park authority has done a good job separating the ski trail system from snowmobiles—and giving skiers nearly 50 miles to themselves. The trail loops are built over the wide, gravel-packed carriage roads. Though ungroomed, most are trackset by previous skiers.

There are loops of just an hour or two, or routes that incorporate a day's skiing through the snow-laden woods, over ice-crusted, gurgling brooks, and into places like Eagle Lake and Jordan Pond. One route takes skiers nearly across to Somes Sound and Northeast Harbor at the seaward end of the peninsula—Maine's Motif Number One. For day skiers who pack a trail lunch and take off, good trail maps are available at the ranger station. Toilet facilities are available near Eagle Lake.

BETHEL INN SKI TOURING CENTER
P.O. Box 49
Bethel, Maine 04217
207-824-2175

Hours: 8 a.m. to 5 p.m.

Trail System: 25 kilometers (about 16 miles).

Trail Difficulty: Easiest, more difficult, most difficult.

Trail Grooming: Yes, on all terrain.

Rental Equipment: Yes.

Instruction: Group and private lessons daily, including Telemarking.

Food Facilities: Main dining room or library open for breakfast and dinner; soups and sandwiches available in the tavern at lunchtime.

Lodging: At the inn.

How to Get There: Maine Turnpike to Exit 11; Route 26 north into Bethel.

The Bethel Inn hardly needs an introduction to aficionados of the rural Northeast. It is a New England classic, its stately colonial yellow dominating the twin-spired Bethel Common. The entire area is in the National Historic District. In summer the inn is a plush country club, in winter a first-rate ski-touring center nestled in the foothills of the White Mountains. Skiers begin right out the back door of the inn, warm up on the golf course, then plunge into the wide, well-marked wooded trails that cross frozen streams and then open into sudden panoramic views of the Longfellow Range. Most trails are made up of gently curving, undulating terrain, just right for beginners and intermediates. However, experts are invited to try their Telemarking technique on Corkscrew or the Peter Grover Hill. The latter is especially steep, and good for Telemark—or Alpine—skiing.

At breakfast, skiers may purchase box lunches for the trail. Our favorite picnic tour is out to the Lake House, where skiers relax and eat in front of the big fieldstone fireplace. Après-ski is casual and friendly—piano bar entertainment on weekends with drinks, sauna, and board games of all kinds.

SUNDAY RIVER SKI TOURING CENTER
RFD 2, Box 1688
Bethel, Maine 04217
207-824-2410

Hours: 9 a.m. to 5 p.m.
Trail System: 40 kilometers (about 25 miles).
Trail Difficulty: Easiest, more difficult, most difficult.
Trail Grooming: 25 kilometers groomed and trackset.
Rental Equipment: Yes.
Instruction: Yes.
Food Facilities: Trail snacks in the touring center; restaurant and lounge within one-half mile access via road or ski trail.
Lodging: At Sunday River Inn, condominiums and rooms, and sleeping bag and dormitory living.
How to Get There: Maine Turnpike to Exit 11 at Gray; Route 26 to Bethel, then Routes 2, 5, and 26 through Bethel to the ski-area access road; signs to the center.

Located in the beautifully wild Sunday River Valley, this touring center offers trails for all abilities and levels of enthusiasm. Beginners enjoy the level terrain in the pine woods near the center, and soon accept the challenge of the 5-mile round trip along the valley floor to Artists' Covered Bridge. Intermediate and expert skiers appreciate the double trackset trails,

and have plenty of challenge with the longer, steeper trails
that meander up and down the rolling hills through mixed
forest growth to the trailside lean-to, the scenic overlook, and
the fabled plunge known as David's Drop. The center offers
night skiing by kerosene lamp on Fridays, citizens' races
through February and March, special events throughout the
winter, and the popular season-transition triathlon, the April
Fools' Day Pole, Paddle, and Paw Race, in late March. Sunday
River is another of those Nordic centers that can take advantage of a well-developed Alpine area.

OAK RIDGE CROSS-COUNTRY SKI AREA
Route 7, Box 2590
Brooks, Maine 04921
207-722-3517

Hours: Friday through Sunday, and holidays, 9 a.m. to 4 p.m.
Trail System: 24 kilometers (about 13 miles).
Trail Difficulty: Easiest, more difficult, most difficult.
Trail Grooming: Groomed and trackset.
Rental Equipment: Yes.
Instruction: Yes.
Food Facilities: Lunches and dinners in Ridge House; Sunday
    brunch from noon to 3 p.m.
Lodging: Motels, bed and breakfast inns in Belfast, 8 miles
    distant.
How to Get There: Maine Turnpike to Augusta, then Route 3 to
    Route 7 in Belfast, Maine, then 6 miles to Brooks; Oak
    Ridge is on the right.

Oak Ridge does not feature races, special events or gimmicks.
Rather, it is an area of serene woodland skiing in the Belfast
Lake Region, with one spectacular view of Camden, Bar Harbor, Blue Mountain, Penobscot Bay, and on a clear day, the
White Mountains. This view is obviously from a highland trail
that winds up for more than 850 feet, crossed by rabbit and
deer tracks, and emerging finally on a plateau with a 360-
degree view of Maine's beauty.

LITTLE LYFORD POND LODGE
Box 688
Brownville, Maine 04414
207-695-2821 (via radio contact)

Hours: Dawn to dusk.
Trail System: About 80 kilometers (50 miles).
Trail Difficulty: Easiest, more difficult, most difficult.
Trail Grooming: Tracked but not groomed.
Rental Equipment: None.
Instruction: Informal.
Food Facilities: Dining in the main lodge.
Lodging: Insulated cabins with woodstoves.
How to Get There: Fly-in service from Greenville, Maine.

Little Lyford is a backcountry destination area for a maximum of ten skiers. For the hearty, rather than flying in, you can ski in over the 10-kilometer trail. Daily touring is in the deep back woods of Maine's north country, over old logging roads and hardwood trails, along frozen stream beds and over hidden ponds. Skiers will visit the spectacular Gulf Hagas Gorge, and break the powder on the surrounding hillsides. The trail network varies from shorter, flatter routes to a challenging trek to the top of Elephant Mountain, or a 13-mile round-trip ski into Greenville. Also available by arrangement are custom inn-to-inn treks. After the daily touring, a sauna awaits tired bodies, and serious country dinners are served at the main lodge. Platform tennis is also available for the tireless.

CARRABASSETT VALLEY RECREATION CENTER
Box 518
Carrabassett Valley, Maine 04947
207-237-2205

Hours: 8:45 a.m. to 4:30 p.m.
Trail System: 105 kilometers (62 miles).
Trail Difficulty: Least difficult, more difficult, most difficult.
Trail Grooming: Most trails groomed as necessary. Some wilderness skiing along the Appalachian Trail.

Rental Equipment: Yes.
Instruction: PSIA-certified.
Food Facilities: Food served weekends and holidays.
Lodging: Inns and motels in the area.
How to Get There: Maine Turnpike to Exit 12 at Auburn; Route
    4 to Farmington, then Route 27 toward Kingfield. The
    touring center is a left turn 14 miles north of Kingfield, 1
    mile from Sugarloaf Mountain, an Alpine area.

This touring area, owned by the town of Carrabassett Valley
(CVRA), is a groomed piece of New England's Big North
Woods, and the place doesn't lose that wild feeling. Indeed,
some of the excursions off the Appalachian trail take skiers
through the cedar bogs frequented by some of the region's
large moose population.

For novice skiers there are the wide, gently graded trails
that run along the old narrow-gauge railroad bed; one favorite
trail runs down along the Carrabassett River nearly to the
door of the famous Red Stallion Inn. For more advanced skiers, the area has a well-marked trail system of steep verticals
and descents through bogs and stream beds. The Touring Center sells good maps, provides rentals and lessons, and offers
all the amenities from hot homemade food to waxing clinics
and moonlight excursions. There is plenty of lodging available
through the Sugarloaf Reservation Service at 207-237-2861.

WESTWAYS ON KEZAR LAKE
Route 5, Box 175
Center Lovell, Maine 04016
207-928-2663

Hours: Daylight.
Trail System: Unlimited wilderness skiing.
Trail Difficulty: Easiest, more difficult, most difficult.
Trail Grooming: No.
Rental Equipment: No.
Instruction: No.
Food Facilities: Breakfast and dinner at the inn Wednesday to
    Sunday; no lunches.

179

Lodging: 7 guest rooms at the inn plus vacation-home rentals on premises.

How to Get There: Maine Turnpike to Route 302 west; Route 5 north for 6 miles to the inn.

Westways skiers look out from the inn on Kezar Lake, where some like to start their skiing either breaking new powder or cruising in tracks of previous skiers. This backs up to West Mountain National Forest, with its dense forestland crossed with old logging roads and paths, many of them groomed by snowmobiles. Here and there are some glimpses of the Presidential Range, as trails roll over small ponds and streams. There is open-terrain skiing for sun-worshipers who prefer to stay in the rolling hills and meadows. The old stone walls and thickets contain rich wildlife throughout the grounds of this 300-acre estate.

The inn itself is the former corporate retreat of the Diamond Match company, and lends guests an après-ski ambiance of rustic elegance and good evening meals. Skiers who want lunch can find food while on the trail into Lovell.

VAL HALLA COUNTRY CLUB AND SKI TOURING CENTER
Val Halla Road
Cumberland, Maine 04021
207-829-3700

Hours: 9 a.m. to 4 p.m.

Trail System: 25 kilometers (about 16 miles).

Trail Difficulty: Easiest, more difficult, most difficult.

Trail Grooming: Yes.

Rental Equipment: Yes.

Instruction: No.

Food Facilities: Snack bar and lounge at the Country Club; full restaurants within 15 miles.

Lodging: Hotels and motels within 10 miles.

How to Get There: Maine Turnpike to Exit 9; Route 1, Tuttle Road, Middle Road, then Greely Road to Val Halla Road.

This touring center is a good example of the growing popularity in country club ski touring. An already established golf facility turns nicely into a ski center with all the amenities, and certainly nice terrain for cross-country runs and tours. Val Halla is in the Casco Bay region of the state, near both Portland and Freeport, the now famous home of L. L. Bean. The skiing itself is gently on the open flats, then rolling in the surrounding woods with streams and ponds. In places the rolling terrain rolls into quite a challenge for skiers of any level.

BEN-LOCH FARM SKI TOURING CENTER
RFD 1, North Road
Dixmont, Maine 04932
207-257-4768

Hours: 10 a.m. to dusk; night tours with headlamps.
Trail System: 34 kilometers (about 19 miles).
Trail Difficulty: Easiest, more difficult, most difficult.
Trail Grooming: Double trackset as needed.
Rental Equipment: 86 sets.
Instruction: Individual and group; videotape sessions.
Food Facilities: Lunchroom at the center; group service by appointment.
Lodging: Bed and breakfast inns and motels within 10 miles.
How to Get There: Maine Turnpike to Exit 42 between Newport and Bangor, Maine; Route 143 east for 3½ miles to the Ben-Loch sign; turn right.

The Ben-Loch Farm Ski Touring Center is a full-scale facility for serious workouts and every level of recreational touring. It offers a well-maintained system of trail loops interlaced through the lovely Dixmont Hills country of east-central Maine. Beginners just getting their pins can stay for a while on the 10-acre field adjacent to the touring center. Here is where the instruction takes place. Then plunge into the 5-kilometer Penobscot Run, an intermediate trail that winds through deep woodlands and around a frozen pond. For the more adventurous, there is the St. John wilderness run or the Kennebec Loop. These are choppy twisters for the advanced skier.

Back at the center, there are a lunchroom and rental and full retail shop that sells knickers, knee socks, hand-knit sweaters and the like. Here, you can sign up for a night ski trip with headlamps, and also pick up one of the best trail maps anywhere.

HOLLEY FARM RESORT
Holley Road
Farmington, Maine 04938
207-778-4869

Hours: 9 a.m. to dusk.
Trail System: 11 kilometers (about 6 miles).
Trail Difficulty: Easiest, more difficult, most difficult.
Trail Grooming: Groomed and double trackset.
Rental Equipment: Yes.
Instruction: By appointment.
Food Facilities: Lunch and dinner at the farm.
Lodging: Several motels in the Farmington area.
How to Get There: Maine Turnpike to Exit 12, then Route 4 north to Farmington; pick up Holley Road for 1 mile to the center.

The field outside the Holley Farm center is a good warm-up for some good woods touring through the hardwood forestland of this region. It is a well-cared-for-system that, although not large, offers good variety and some excellent training tracks. A race program is being developed for the area, and all levels of recreational tourers will find comfortable ski surroundings here. The area also offers pool, sauna, restaurant, and lounge.

TITCOMB MOUNTAIN SKI TOURING CENTER
Morrison Hill Road
Farmington, Maine 04938
207-778-9031

Hours: Tuesday through Friday, 1 to 4 p.m.; Saturday and Sunday, 9 a.m. to 4 p.m.
Trail System: 25 kilometers (about 15 miles).
Trail Difficulty: Easiest, more difficult, most difficult.
Trail Grooming: Yes.
Rental Equipment: Nearby in Farmington.
Instruction: Yes.
Food Facilities: Lunch available at the lodge; several restaurants nearby.
Lodging: Several inns and motels in the area.
How to Get There: Maine Turnpike to the Auburn, Maine, exit; Route 4 north to Farmington.

In the foothills of the Longfellow Mountains in west-central Maine, the Titcomb trails—mostly beginner and intermediate—roll over gentle hills and through meadows and fir forest. The trail system accesses an additional 15 miles of trails in the woods, one of them leading to a downtown restaurant in this pretty college-campus town. Through the Farmington Ski Club, Titcomb offers citizen racing, ski jumping, and Telemark practice on the nearby Alpine area. The large lodge has a lunch counter, rest rooms, and changing and waxing rooms. Lessons are given each afternoon, by appointment.

TROLL VALLEY LODGE SKI TOURING CENTER
16 Stewart Avenue
Farmington, Maine 04938
207-778-2830

Hours: Dawn to dusk.
Trail System: 15 kilometers (about 9 miles).
Trail Difficulty: Mostly easiest, more difficult; some most difficult.

183

Trail Grooming: Groomed and double trackset.
Rental Equipment: Yes.
Instruction: Yes.
Food Facilities: Lunch counter at the center. Full restaurants in Farmington.
Lodging: Hotels and motels within 1 mile.
How to Get There: Maine Turnpike to Auburn, Maine; Route 4 to the Colonial motel, 2 miles before Farmington. Left at the Red School House, then 1 mile to the center.

Troll Valley is a rolling valley between two high hills in this west-central Maine college town. This is a high-energy place with lots of racing, racing talk, racing clubs, and the like. Interconnected with the Titcomb Mountain Alpine area, there is also Telemarking instruction and practice. The terrain ranges from open rolling flats to woods trails that course out around a beaver bog, through hardwood and pine forest land. Beyond the groomed trails, there is access to unlimited skiing on the ungroomed logging roads of the surrounding forest. The center has rental and retail equipment available, and serves light food and trail snacks.

CRAB APPLE INN
The Forks, Maine 04985
207-663-2218

Hours: No set hours.
Trail System: About 95 kilometers (about 55 miles).
Trail Difficulty: Easiest, more difficult, most difficult.
Trail Grooming: None, except by snowmobiles that use the area.
Rental Equipment: None.
Instruction: No.
Food Facilities: Breakfast and dinner by reservation at the inn; lunch snacks at the nearby general store.
Lodging: 7 rooms at the inn; housekeeping cottage.
How to Get There: Maine Turnpike to Exit 36; Route 201 for 62 miles to The Forks.

Overlooking a dramatic sweep of the Kennebec River, Crab Apple Inn offers seven rooms as well as a guest house with housekeeping privileges. This is North Country skiing in the true sense of that term, as the old logging roads here criss-cross infinitely, it seems, through deep wilderness forest, along the river valley, and up over mountain ridges along the trail that Benedict Arnold marched his troops to Quebec. That wonderful city, incidentally, is just 140 miles from the inn.

Everyone at some point should have the experience of skiing into Moxie Falls—the highest waterfall in New England—or explore The Forks itself, a point of land at the confluence of the Dead and Kennebec rivers. Available from the inn are guided backcountry tours where trekkers cannot help but run across snowshoe hare, deer, and moose signs. This is not for experts only, by the way, as the riverside trails along the Kennebec are gentle, and groomed out by snowmobiles. This is true New England wilderness skiing several light years from civilization.

CHESUNCOOK LAKE WILDERNESS TOURING
Chesuncook Village
Route 75
Greenville, Maine 04441
207-695-2821 (Folsom's Flying Service)

Hours: By arrangement.
Trail System: Infinite.
Trail Difficulty: Easiest, more difficult, most difficult.
Trail Grooming: No.
Rental Equipment: No.
Instruction: In tour groups only.
Food Facilities: Dinner only.
Lodging: Housekeeping cabins are available and well equipped; bring sleeping bags and food.
How to Get There: No auto access; visitors must ski, sled, or fly in; make contact through Folsom's Flying Service.

Chesuncook is another of the prime wilderness ski-guide outfitters that can put together an outback trek for all tastes and

abilities of skiing. The Chesuncook Lake House Lodge and
Cabins is a well-established fishing complex in the remote uplands of central Maine. In winter, Chesuncook offers the serious skier an opportunity to enjoy the solitude and seclusion of
the Northern Maine experience. This is a remote, primitive
area for advanced skiers, or for those folks flexible enough to
approach such an experience with respect, understanding,
and foresight. Skiers who do are rewarded with the truly
amazing experiences of this country, from the "quiet beauty of
the sun igniting the ice crystals on Baxter Peak in the early
morn, to the pristine solitude of a snow-covered landscape
with the vast open spaces of the frozen lakes ..."—lines
penned by a frequent skier at Chesuncook. It may not be so
easy to reach, but that is part of the charm. For real wilderness skiing, it's worth the hassle of getting here.

SQUAW MOUNTAIN SKI TOURING CENTER
Box D
Greenville, Maine 04441
207-695-2272

Hours: Dawn to dusk.
Trail System: 45 kilometers (about 28 miles).
Trail Difficulty: Easiest, more difficult, most difficult.
Trail Grooming: 15 kilometers groomed and trackset; unlim-
    ited wilderness skiing.
Rental Equipment: Yes.
Instruction: Yes.
Food Facilities: Lunches in the cafeteria, with lunches and
    dinners in main lodge.
Lodging: 55 separate units in the main lodge; the bunkroom
    sleeps 40 dormitory-style.
How to Get There: I-95 to Newport, Maine; Route 7 north to
    Dexter; Route 23 north to Guilford; Routes 6 and 15 north
    to Greenville; signs to Squaw Mountain.

Though remote, the Squaw Mountain Touring Center shares
the complete facilities of the Alpine area, and so skiers here
can enjoy après-ski hours in relative luxury. The interlacing

trail loops cover 45 kilometers, with nearly limitless possibilities encompassed in the trails and logging roads that maze throughout the Moosehead Lake Region. One loop goes across and around the frozen water; another leads skiers up to a wonderful panoramic overlook of this huge lake. Then a call to Dick Folsom at Folsom's Flying Service in Greenville will get you a fly-in ski trek to the Allagash or Baxter areas for some remote wilderness skiing. At Squaw itself, Telemarking and Alpine are also available, as are all the amenities of rental, retail, food, and lounging facilities.

SPRUCE MOUNTAIN SKI TOURING CENTER
RFD 2, Box 8425
Jay, Maine 04239
207-645-4630 or 207-897-2121 days

Hours: Weekdays 3 p.m. to 5 p.m.; weekends 8 a.m. to 5 p.m.
Trail System: 7½ kilometers (about 5 miles).
Trail Difficulty: Easiest, more difficult, most difficult.
Trail Grooming: Groomed and trackset.
Rental Equipment: No.
Instruction: No.
Food Facilities: At the Alpine hill.
Lodging: In the Farmington area or Lewiston area, within 10 to 18 miles.
How to Get There: Maine Turnpike to Exit 12; Route 4 north, turn right before the bridge into Livermore Falls. The center is a half mile down the river.

Spruce Mountain is a small area run in conjunction with the Spruce Mountain Alpine area on the West Bank of the Androscoggin River. When the Alpine slopes are in operation, a snack bar is available. The trails vary in length and difficulty, from rolling riverside roadways to some challenging up and down loops that combine Alpine trails for Telemarking.

WINTER'S INN SKI TOURING CENTER
Box 44
Kingfield, Maine 04947
207-265-5421

Hours: 9 a.m. to dusk.
Trail System: 30 kilometers (about 19 miles).
Trail Difficulty: Easiest, more difficult.
Trail Grooming: No.
Rental Equipment: Yes.
Instruction: No.
Food Facilities: Breakfast and dinner at the inn; lunches within skiing distance of the center.

Lodging: Winter's Inn has 12 rooms; several motels and inns in the area.

How to Get There: Maine Turnpike to the second Augusta exit; Route 27 north to Kingfield.

Here, in one of the dramatic mountain areas in the Northeast—the Bigelow Range overlooking the Carrabassett Valley—Winter's Inn sits on a small hilltop overlooking the village of Kingfield. This restored Victorian country mansion was originally designed by the Stanley Brothers who invented the Stanley Steamer. It has five working fireplaces, a genial atmosphere, and plenty of art objects and antiques to look at. Various views from the inn overlook Bigelow, Mt. Abrams, and Mt. Blue, as well as one of New England's true classic Alpine areas, Sugarloaf/USA.

Skiers have nearly limitless terrain at their disposal on wilderness trails carved from old logging roads, down through pine glades to the West Branch of the Carrabassett River. Here the wildlife is abundant, the skiing varied and vigorous. There is also open-field skiing through gently rolling uplands. For Telemark aficionados, Sugarloaf has plenty of terrain both gentle and steep. This big-country region can be skied season after season without giving up all her secrets and surprises to skiers.

MOUNT ABRAM SKI TOURING
Box 193
Locke Mills, Maine 04255
207-875-2601

Hours: 9 a.m. to 4 p.m.
Trail System: 20 kilometers (about 12 miles).
Trail Difficulty: Easiest, more difficult, most difficult.
Trail Grooming: Groomed and trackset.
Rental Equipment: Yes.
Instruction: By appointment.
Food Facilities: Cafeteria for lunches in the lodge.
Lodging: In Bethel or West Paris, about 10 miles distant.

How to Get There: Maine Turnpike to Exit 11, then Route 26 to
   Locke Mills.

Mt. Abram's Ski Touring center is nestled beside Alpine
slopes, allowing skiers to make use of Telemark terrain, as
well as the skier facilities already there. After skiing along the
base of the downhill slopes, tourers plunge into the snow-
laden hardwood and pine trails, following old logging roads,
stream beds, and over small bridges criss-crossing Putt Brook.
This is picturesque terrain, easy to negotiate, though there are
some challenging climbs, twists, turns, and descents on some
of the trails. Moonlight tours are available along a wide trail,
and citizen races are encouraged here, including the annual
Bob Cole Cup Race.

BAXTER STATE PARK
64 Balsam Drive
Millinocket, Maine 04462
207-723-5140

Hours: Daylight, December through March.
Trail System: Wilderness trails over 100 square miles.
Trail Difficulty: Easiest, more difficult, most difficult.
Trail Grooming: None.
Rental Equipment: No.
Instruction: No.
Food Facilities: In Millinocket, about 25 miles distant.
Lodging: In Millinocket.
How to Get There: I-95 to Millinocket, then Greenville Road to
   the Baxter State Park entrance 18 miles past town.

Though Baxter State Park is on a well-worn path of Maine's
summertime delights, in winter, it is a remote wildland of
fierce weather and tough outdoor challenges. Thus, touring
here should be considered only by the most experienced
woodsman-skier who has a working knowledge of what winter
means in this deep northern country. Though the skiing itself
need not be the hairiest, especially with the miles of flattish

logging roads between Millinocket and Greenville, winter camping is available in a limited number of bunkhouses, lean-tos, tents, and igloos. Skiers must either bushwhack in to the Park Headquarters, or take the Golden Road, sharing it with lumber carriers bringing pulp wood to the mill.

All the caveats aside, however, this is wonderful back-woods country along one of the most spectacular water-courses in the Northeast—the West Branch of the Penobscot River. The snow-covered bulk of Mt. Katahdin looms over the land (it may not be climbed in winter, incidentally). For skiers who want truly to break away from the crowds, and who are confident of their outdoor skills, Baxter State Park is among the finest wilderness ski expeditions to be found anywhere.

KATAHDIN LAKE WILDERNESS CAMPS
Box 389
Millinocket, Maine 04462

Hours: Daily, dawn to dusk.
Trail System: 48 kilometers (about 30 miles).
Trail Difficulty: More difficult, most difficult wilderness trails.
Trail Grooming: No.
Rental Equipment: No.
Instruction: No.
Food Facilities: Yes.
Lodging: At the camp center and camps.
How to Get There: I-95 to Route 157 to Millinocket Lake. Here,
     either fly-in or ski-in access; there is no auto road.

On the remote shores of Katahdin Lake, these wilderness camps are the gateway to real outback trekking experience. Like many such guided tours, skiing skill and experience are not the critical factors. Rather, Katahdin's tours are for adven-turous folks in fairly good physical shape who are flexible enough to trade amenities for stunning wilderness adventure. Being in decent shape, though, is a starter.

The tour begins with a fly-in (or ski-in) to the camps along the frozen shore of the beautiful Katahdin Lake, about 30 miles north of Millinocket. If you ski from the lake, where you'll leave your car, to the camps, it is full-day, 20-mile trek. However, Scotty's Flying Service at Shin Pond will be happy to take you in. It takes about 12 minutes by plane.

At the camp center there are American Plan accommodations with family-style meals. Aside from this there are no rental or retail goods available, so skiers must bring what is necessary for a few days of trekking—from clothes and equipment to waxes. One tip: Bring a camera. You'll be touring in some of the most astounding backcountry anywhere, a place where "the only nightlife you will hear will be a distant owl or coyote in the hills," in the words of director Al Cooper. In the morning the tracks of a grouse, moose, or pine marten crossing your trail may tell you you are not completely alone in this beautiful winter world.

CARTER'S FARM MARKET SKI TOURING CENTER
Route 26
Oxford, Maine 04270
207-539-4848

Hours: 9 a.m. to 5 p.m. Night skiing on weekends.
Trail System: 10 kilometers (about 6 miles).
Trail Difficulty: Easiest, more difficult.
Trail Grooming: Groomed and trackset.
Rental Equipment: Yes.
Instruction: Yes.
Food Facilities: Trail snacks at center; restaurants within a few miles.
Lodging: Motels in South Paris and Otisfield, about 7 miles distant.
How to Get There: Maine Turnpike through Portland, Maine, to Exit 11 at Gray. Route 100 to Route 26 north. The farm is about 12 miles from Gray.

So many of the most pleasant New England touring centers have been established on working farms, and this one is in that tradition. Carter's Farm Market is a summer produce operation which, once the snow flies, turns its gently rolling pastureland and woods into a full-scale touring center. The retail/rental facility is well stocked with skis, clothing, and equipment, and the lounge is a friendly place to relax and talk about what wax you should have used.

The trails at Carter Farm are varied, from open-field cruisers and racing courses, to one lovely solitude tour along the Androscoggin River. Hogan's Pond is another pretty destination for a daily tour. At the Carters', citizen races are run throughout the season, along with junior programs and a Winter Carnival. Night skiing is also a fun feature of the area. David Carter, director of the area, is a cross-country skier of 20 years' experience who set up the Jackson Touring Center for Eastern Mountain Sports. When it comes to running a touring center, Carter knows what he is about.

SUMMIT SPRINGS SKI TOURING CENTER
Box 455
Poland Spring, Maine 04274
207-647-3603

Hours: Dawn to dusk.
Trail System: 12 kilometers (about 7 miles).
Trail Difficulty: Easiest, more difficult, most difficult.
Trail Grooming: Double trackset.
Rental Equipment: Yes.
Instruction: Yes.
Food Facilities: Snack bar at the center plus restaurants in Poland Spring.
Lodging: None at the center; motels in Poland Spring.
How to Get There: Maine Turnpike to Exit 12; north on Route 4 for a half mile, then left and follow into Poland Spring.

Summit Springs Ski Touring Center is on the site of an ancient mansion that once stood on this hilltop overlooking a 360-degree vista of surrounding gladed valleys and the distant White Mountains. Trails blossom out through woods, along old roads, and eventually wind down to Tripp Lake with its wonderful mountain view and shoreside trail loop. The center itself bustles with a rental/retail operation where you can sign up for lessons, citizen races, and ski-week activities; the center has a wax room and a snack bar.

COUNTRY CLUB INN–
EDELWEISS SKI TOURING CENTER
Box 680, Country Club Drive
Rangeley, Maine 04970
207-864-3831

Hours: 9 a.m. to dusk.
Trail System: 5 kilometers (about 3 miles) of maintained trails; unlimited wilderness terrain.
Trail Difficulty: Easiest, more difficult.
Trail Grooming: Most trackset and groomed.
Rental Equipment: Yes.
Instruction: No.
Food Facilities: Dining room at the center for breakfast and dinner; restaurants in Rangeley Center, 2 miles distant.
Lodging: 25 rooms.
How to Get There: Maine Turnpike to Route 4 at Auburn, Maine, then to Rangeley; left at Mingo Springs; north out of Rangeley Village to the inn.

Rangeley, Maine, is one of the sweet corners of the earth. A trout mecca nestled into the valleys of the Bigelow Range in the west-central region of the state, Rangeley is a land of thick fir and hardwood forest and broad lakes. Though there is an Alpine ski area (Saddleback) nearby, this is still unspoiled country well away from the crush of weekenders; it is, however, a favorite snowmobile region. Leaving the Country Club Inn, trails begin on a golf course that overlooks the white expanse of Rangeley Lake, then they plunge into the timberland and roll through the gentle hills with clearings giving sudden glimpses of Saddleback, Sugarloaf, and Bigelow mountains. It is not uncommon to come upon moose and deer tracks in this wilderness, and the skiing along old logging roads and stream beds is, literally, limitless. Next stop, Quebec. Back at the inn, several fireplaces and a hot buttered rum take the chill off and soothe weary muscles, before a big, home-cooked meal is served in the dining room.

SADDLEBACK   .
Box 490
Rangeley, Maine 04970
207-864-3380

Hours: 9 a.m. to 4 p.m.
Trail System: 40 kilometers (about 25 miles).
Trail Difficulty: Easiest, more difficult, most difficult.
Trail Grooming: As needed.
Rental Equipment: Yes.
Instruction: PSIA-certified instructors.
Food Facilities: Available at the Saddleback Mountain base lodge.
Lodging: Condominiums available at the mountain; inns and motels in the town nearby.
How to Get There: Maine Turnpike to Exit 12 in Auburn, Maine; Route 4 north to Rangeley; follow signs to Saddleback and the touring facility.

As an Alpine area, Saddleback is rightfully dubbed New England's best-kept secret. The same can be said for the Nordic touring center, and the region generally. It is a land of broad lakes—Rangeley, Saddleback, and Mooselookmeguntik—and trout streams that course out of the Bigelow Mountains, whose peaks command views of the entire region. Despite the beauty of the area and a base elevation (2,500 feet) that ensures a much longer-than-average ski season, the Rangeley region is uncrowded and unhurried. This is a perfect area to combine a Nordic-Alpine ski vacation, or to make use of Saddleback Mountain's easier Alpine trails for your Telemark work. The 40 kilometers of carefully groomed and trackset trails combine all the terrain, from gentle rolling tours along the lake shore, and across the lake expanse, to stiff climbs up the flank of Saddleback Mountain itself. One reward for this

climb is a truly stunning view of Saddleback Lake followed by a gentle meandering descent down the Lazy River trail. Then follow this with an après-ski hour in the Painted Pony, Saddleback's rollicking lounge upstairs at the baselodge. A full cafeteria operates daily here, and serves a homemade chili that must, hands down, take top chili honors in all of ski land.

THE BIRCHES SKI TOURING CENTER
Rockwood, Maine 04478
207-534-7305

Hours: Dawn to dusk.
Trail System: 40 kilometers (25 miles).
Trail Difficulty: Easiest, more difficult, most difficult.
Trail Grooming: Groomed and trackset as needed.
Rental Equipment: Yes.
Instruction: PSIA-certified.
Food Facilities: Restaurant in Rockwood Center, 2 miles from the center.
Lodging: Several cabins and lodges in the area.
How to Get There: I-95 to Newport, Maine, then Route 7 north to Dexter; Route 23 north to Guilford; pick up Routes 6 and 15 through the town of Greenville around the lake to Rockwood; cross the Moose River and follow a logging road to center.

Looking for wilderness ski trips? Overnights? Fly-ins to the wild backcountry of the Northeast? Here it is. Maine's big North Woods is the closest thing in New England to rival Michigan's Upper Peninsula. This is not intended to scare off less-experienced skiers, but simply to remind potential visitors that outback trekking in this countryside requires forethought, planning, and investigation. That said, the rewards of skiing The Birches are immense, and the sport enters an entirely new dimension.

The center itself overlooks Mt. Kineo, and skiers can be content to stay on the 40 kilometers of groomed, trackset trails along the picturesque western shore of the lake. Rental and retail shop, along with hot drink and sandwiches, is available. For the adventurous, The Birches operates in conjunction with North Country Outfitters, and can plan a multi-day trek for skiers whose only requirement is good health and a willing heart. No experience is necessary, in other words. You will be in the hands of professional guides and instructors who will lead the tour through these stupendous backlands, leaving 2,000-foot towers like Elephant and Indian mountains at your back. During the day, you'll ski from inn to inn along old logging roads and woodland trails; late in the afternoon you'll be ready to relax around a warm stove before the big home-cooked dinner at the inn.

For the ultimate New England trek, The Birches offers a backpacking tour to Chimney Pond at the base of mile-high Mt. Katahdin. By day you'll be working over Alpine terrain—rock faces, ice falls, and snow fields. You'll learn the basics of winter mountaineering, and ski the lower snow bowls of the majestic Katahdin. This trip requires both physical and mental stamina, though not great skiing experience. The adventure is well worth the effort.

BLACK MOUNTAIN OF MAINE

50 Congress Street
Rumford, Maine 04276
207-364-8977

Hours: Dawn to dusk.
Trail System: 15 kilometers (about 9 miles).
Trail Difficulty: Easiest, more difficult, most difficult.
Trail Grooming: Groomed and trackset.
Rental Equipment: Nearby in Rumford.
Instruction: Yes.
Food Facilities: A lunch counter at the center.
Lodging: In Rumford.
How to Get There: Maine Turnpike north to Auburn; Route 4 to
    Livermore; Route 108 to Rumford.

Black Mountain of Maine is a medium-sized area in the central range of the state, near an Alpine ski area and ski-jumping complex. The trail system was intelligently designed by Chammy Broomhall, designer of the Olympic trail system at Lake Placid and Squaw Valley, and still a vital part of the competitive Nordic scene. Black Mountain reflects this dedication to quality cross-country skiing on every level, from first-time-out novices to racers training for a Ski Chase marathon.

Epilogue: One of Too Few Days

It was nearly 4 a.m. and the wind was down. Whatever had woken me—there were mice in this place, we knew—was still now. I went over to the window and pulled back the wool blanket we had tacked against the cold early last evening. When we turned in, a storm was raging across the valley, so the window was just a flat black. But sometime in the night the weather had blown itself out. Now over the still silver landscape hung a solemn January moon. I knew in a few hours one of Those Days was going to dawn.

There are too few such days in a winter; too few in a lifetime. The world remade by new snow, bright sun in an endless sky (for the high pressure was surely locked in for a while) and no commitment beyond a full day's skiing. It would be perfect. Even anticipating such a day, knowing how brief and finite it would be, brought a peculiar sense of dread to underline the exhilaration as I stood there at the window. I thought thoughts that look grotesquely sentimental on paper:

"This would be a day to be tuned to every minute, to resist that all-too-human habit of blocking off the senses, of losing awareness so that hours of light slip by uncounted, practically unnoticed.

"That may be okay back in the work world, sitting in commuter traffic or something of the kind. But not this day. This day would be perfect, every minute of it to be turned over and over, examined, savored."

Three hours later the moon was down and the first streak of hard orange light slashed across the peak of Bald Mountain. Bacon and coffee smells filled the cabin; over twenty years of marriage, these two chores—the spadework of our vacation breakfasts—have fallen to me. Then Lyn, the superstar surgeon who can flip fried eggs without breaking them, steps in for the artistic work.

You can eat a big breakfast before a day of skiing, for the sport burns calories like none other I know. We were staying

at a friend's camp in central Maine, and the plan was to ski twelve miles to a village at the far shore of the lake, then cross the lake for the four-mile shot home. After breakfast, as Lyn packed a trail lunch, I went about the ceremonial business of determining the wax of the day.

I have been with ski groups who delight in arguing all through breakfast about waxing, various members going out every five minutes to stick a thermometer in sunlit snow, then in the shady snow, then to stand around ruminatively stroking the chin while pretending to know a great deal about winter. My own experience is that for recreational touring you can be a color or so off to the cold side, and it really won't matter much, especially if your touch on the skis is right. All it will really mean is that you herringbone uphill a little sooner than you would otherwise. And you can be more than a color off to the warm side before you start clogging up your kick zone.

I used some paint thinner to remove some old grip wax from the green glider base we'd ironed on the fiberglass bottoms at the beginning of the season, then on the kick zone I smeared on some green grip wax—just a guess on my part at which would be a good start in this dry, fluffy stuff.

Anyway, as long as waxing stays ceremonial, it is fun. So
the skis were prepared on our perfect morning, lunch, waxes,
extra clothes packed in the back pack, and off we went.

The empty woods on a cold morning ring with quiet. The
powder was still unbroken as we made our way up behind the
cabin, mounting toward a high ridge that ran for about three
miles overlooking the lake. The only break in the trail were the
delicate strings of beads, the tracks of small animals—squir-
rels, snowshoe hare, voles, and the like—up and busy in these
hills long before us. During a blizzard deer will hunker down
in the snow and become buried for the duration. When they
sense the storm's end, they will break out to continue their
ceaseless winter foraging for food, and you sometimes come
upon their tracks winter mornings after a snowfall. You are
reminded that Northern New England is the extreme range of
whitetail deer; in the deepest months the animals are always
in peril.

As you stretch out, skiing faster through the dark hollows
and over small rises—always ascending—the muscles work
out, and the stiffness of beginning is gone. Skiing becomes
easier. You are in rhythm, and are aware of your sound, skis
patting, then gliding on the snow, your breath coming out in
plumes as your lungs work to drink the winter-cold oxygen.
Rhythm, the slash-slash of skis, the steamy breath, and suddenly you become aware of how loud the sound of your skiing
is in this early silence.

Still in shade, we made one slight descent, then turned
uphill again through a stand of birch and snow-laden fir
boughs. I chose one route up here; Lyn said she would skirt
around through another likely looking road that would be
better going, and would meet me at the other side of a knoll I
was already ascending.

"I think my way's shorter," I told her.

"It's too thick-looking up there. I'm taking the road," she
said, and we parted company.

I was determined to get over that knoll then ski back
down to the road, to be waiting there not even breathing hard,

as if I'd been there for half the morning when she showed up. Skiing harder up toward the rise, I had to duck under several branches so heavily laden they looked ready to snap. As my shoulder brushed by, unburdening them, the boughs sprung one by one toward the sky, spraying me with powder.

Toward the top of a mountain ridge, summer or winter, when you emerge from thick woods to a spacious overlook, there is a sense of climbing out a skylight onto the roof of the world. Here, abruptly, I was in sunlight, full and dazzling. Far below the lake spread out for ten miles, a pool of spilled milk. Beyond one shore, the tiny village stoked its fires in the cold morning, the thin curls of smoke rising from every rooftop into the valley air. Even farther beyond the lake and village rose another mountain ridge, then another a fainter blue behind it, and another behind that. Looking out over mountain ranges, you see the tumultuous energy of a frozen ocean. And as far as I could see, perhaps eighty miles, just visible behind the last ridge rose the oddly sinister white bulk of Mount Katahdin.

It was some time before I noticed there was no way down from where I stood. The underbrush among the firs down the sunny side of the ridge was waist-high and so thick there was no apparent opening. But I was not about to backtrack to the road, then skirt all the way around, following Lyn by perhaps fifteen minutes. I drove down through the underbrush and commenced such a fight with the thickets that after ten minutes or so I was more amused than irritated. I would finally hack an opening, make a move through it to find that my ski was hung up around a stalk or some creeper vines, so that I was forced to back up again to free the ski, then look to the other one to see what it was doing. Meanwhile, I had to duck under the heavy fir boughs that kept dumping their powder over my shoulders and head. Just as I was losing a ridiculous battle with these woods, I was at last free, and worked down to the road. As I arrived, snowcovered, disheveled, steaming and panting from the effort, there was Lyn looking as if she'd been waiting there all morning. No explanation was necessary. "How's the other guy look?" she asked.

We found a patch of sunlight to stop in. After two hours of skiing, it was time to shed a layer, have some coffee and

Hershey chunks, before pushing on to our lunch stop. We descended half a mile to the lake. Where the downhill run was clear, it was exhilarating, for we could let out the skis as fast as we could travel through powder, then slow down naturally as the terrain leveled. But it did occur to me that going downhill on skinny skis is not as much fun as going up gentle climbs, or over flats. And this is a matter of sheer skiing skill, or lack thereof: You can learn to charge over flats and pump uphill and get the same exhilarating high that distance runners feel. But the ability to ride a ski downhill with confidence through twisting terrain and switchbacks, that is a matter of years and miles under the skis. For that there is no substitute.

Our lunch was hot soup from a wide-mouth Thermos, chicken chunks, bread, cheese, and wine to wash it down. Now the sun was high and flooded into our small clearing. I peeled off a layer and sat there steaming, pointing my face stupidly to the sky. Odd, wasn't it? Here in the heart of winter—the darkest month in one of the fiercest climates in North America—it was possible to peel off layers of clothing, sip wine, and nearly doze in the sunshine. But shadows begin to elongate quickly on a January day. After half an hour or so there was a sudden nudge of urgency. Get going. We picked up, smeared a touch of blue wax over the green, and were off again, feeling stiff and cranky, along the shore of the lake.

We were getting near civilization now. The first sign was the waste of raw material from which the outlanders—beavers—had built winter communes. They had built two huge lodges just offshore of the lake, and all along the shore lay the ruins of birch trees they had felled for the construction. A wasteful project, this, for the beavers used only medium logs and small limbs, leaving the greater part of the tree sprawled on the forest floor to rot. And how much more wasteful, it seems, when the waste is birch. Scattered among these stands of beech, maple, and birch, were silver birches, the prettiest trees I have seen, their trunks shining a bright gold-bronze color, bright as polished metal in the chilly sunlight.

We passed out of beaver country and began coming upon that most common of lodgings in ski country, the ubiquitous, inevitable condominium. With the first ones we passed, we knew, despite the last part of our trip ahead of us—a straight shot home across the lake after picking up groceries—The Day was at its end.

And the run home, our dividend, was nearly uneventful except for the hugest of events. Two of them.

Loaded down with two extra packs stuffed with all kinds of unnecessaries for the rest of our week up-country, we headed back across the lake just as the sun diffused in that broad florid band across the western sky, an unconvincing final show of force before the winter night shut down over all light once again. It was comfortable on the lake. There was no wind. Skiers had left behind plenty of tracks for us to get into and cruise along, and the dropping of temperatures made the surface firm and fast. And again there was the exhilaration of the aerobic rhythm, the rhythm of motion and breathing, that slash-slash of the skis. We were across in no time.

We ascended the opposite banking crossing a neighbor's meadow in the dark, then up past his barn where a solitary white cat dozed on a window ledge under the outside light.

Then into the dark again, through more trees to the last field we would have to cross to get back to our cabin. At the edge of the clearing there was movement of some kind. Startled, I stared at something large and dark moving against the trees. The movement was not rushed, but slow and weighty. I was stunned. I tried to focus on an oft-repeated belief of an old Vermonter who taught me how to fly-fish: "The only animal you have to worry about in the New England woods stands on two legs."

Then I thought the neighbor's cows were loose, or perhaps horses. But the apparition finally resolved itself into a couple of moose sauntering along at the edge of the woods. If our sudden presence stirred them into motion, they certainly were not hurried about anything now. Their heads looking naked without antlers—the winter style for these thousand-pound monsters—they slowly shuffled toward the trees. Moose are the only creatures in New England for whom winter absolutely does not exist. I have seen them from an airplane lying on their backs and wriggling back and forth like horses in summer mud. Where the whitetailed deer are constantly threatened up here, these huge cousins do not even feel the pinch.

We heard their hooves plunge lazily a few times, then the noise stopped. The moose had stopped just a few yards into the trees, and would wait for us to pass on before coming back to the clearing. It is no wonder hunters have a 90-percent success ratio up here with these brutes.

We crossed the last field, slowly and sorely now; day's end was suddenly long overdue. Halfway across the field we could see that the friends we'd expected sometime that evening had already arrived and were waiting for us. The windows were full of light. You could see wood smoke from the chimney against the stars.

Index to Skiing Sites

About the Authors

Outdoor and ski editor for the *Boston Globe* since 1980, Tony Chamberlain is a veteran skier who has been on the slopes and breaking trails for more than twenty years. His articles on various aspects of skiing have appeared in *Skiing*, *Powder*, and *Yankee* magazines.

Lyn Chamberlain, a writer and former reporter, is also an avid skier. Together Lyn and Tony have enjoyed exploring the many ski areas of New England, often accompanied by their son, Christopher.

Other titles of interest from **The Globe Pequot Press**:

Guidebooks:
Guide to the Recommended Country Inns of New England
Budget Dining and Lodging in New England
Daytrips and Budget Vacations in New England
Bed and Breakfast in the Northeast
The Handbook for Beach Strollers from Maine
  to Cape Hatteras

"Short Walks" books:
. . . *in Connecticut*
. . . *on Long Island*
. . . *on Cape Cod and the Vineyard*

"Short Bike Rides" books:
. . . *on Long Island*
. . . *in Rhode Island*
. . . *in the Berkshires*
. . . *on Cape Cod, Nantucket, and the Vineyard*
. . . *in Connecticut*
. . . *in Greater Boston and Central Massachusetts*

Three-Volume Set of "Traveling and Camping in the National
Park Areas"
Western States
Eastern States
Mid-America

Available at your bookstore or direct from the publisher. For a
free catalogue or to place an order, call 1-800-243-0495 (in
Connecticut, 1-800-962-0973) or write: The Globe Pequot Press,
Old Chester Road, Box Q, Chester, Connecticut 06412.